The New Poor

Contemporary Issues Series

The New Poor

Anatomy of Underprivilege

edited by Ian Henderson

PETER OWEN · LONDON

ISBN 0 7206 0200 9

PETER OWEN LIMITED
20 Holland Park Avenue London W11 3QU

First British Commonwealth edition 1973
© Peter Owen Ltd 1973

Printed in Great Britain by
Bristol Typesetting Co Ltd
Barton Manor St Philips Bristol

To DES WILSON

They live isolated on a lonely island of
poverty in an ocean of material prosperity

(DR MARTIN LUTHER KING JNR)

Contents

Being Poor

Being poor is washing in an old tin bath
Being poor is losing and not knowing how to laugh
Being poor is freezing with no coal for the hearth
That's what being poor is

Being poor is paying rent three weeks late
Being poor is eating off a dirty tin plate
Being poor is dirtiness and clothes in a state
That's what being poor is

Being poor is watching others go on holiday
Being poor is staying in on a Saturday
Being poor is a hovel with rooms in disarray
That's what being poor is

Being poor is stale bread, bad cheese and rancid butter
Being poor is dog-ends taken from the gutter
Being poor is dysentery, coughs, colds and splutters
That's what being poor is

Being poor is knowing just how far dole money goes
Being poor is plastic daffs and not a real rose
Being poor is coat sleeves to wipe a runny nose
That's what being poor is

David Dalton
(Westminster City School)

Introduction

The Changed Face of Poverty

The Times was positively euphoric. In a 1951 leader it spoke rapturously of 'no less than the virtual abolition of sheerest want'. The occasion for this rejoicing was the publication in that year of the third and final survey on poverty, conducted by the indefatigable Seebohm Rowntree and G. R. Lavers and based on the city of York. Rowntree and Lavers had shocked the nation ten years earlier in 1941, by revealing that in 1936 18 per cent of York's population lived in poverty. Now, in 1951, they reported that this figure had been reduced to one and a half per cent.[1]

Throughout the 1950s the euphoria persisted. Even left-wing politicians turned their attention to other causes, such as nuclear disarmament, and the misgivings felt in 1959 about Macmillan's 'Never had it so good' speech (which, to be fair, was misquoted) were based on moral rather than factual grounds. There had of course been real gains. Two factors, apart from the boost given to the economy by the war, contributed most. One was the virtual annihilation of mass unemployment due to the discovery and application of Keynesian economics. The other was the creation of the Welfare State.

One interesting feature of the period was the re-orientation of goals and techniques in social work, and the tendency to explain social problems in terms of psychology rather than economics. Coates and Silburn wrote in 1970 :

The fifties were the heyday of what is now referred to as the 'psychiatric deluge' in social work training programmes. During this period social casework was seen as a form of intensive social therapy, concentrating on revealing the 'latent' personality problems which underlie such 'manifest' symptoms as shortage of money. Heavily influenced by ideas borrowed from psychoanalysis, social work theory emphasized the essential individuality of each client's problems; thus by their training, social workers were encouraged to interpret all public ills as personal problems and saw their role as helping each client to adjust to the 'realities' of his environment.[2]

A seminal work which was both a product of the 1950s and an influential factor in revising judgements about poverty was an American contribution. J. K. Galbraith's *The Affluent Society*[3] made the now-famous comparison between 'public squalor and private affluence'. Galbraith based his essay on an appreciation of the dramatic social changes brought about by full employment and welfare. He did however cast doubt upon the 'conventional wisdom' which decreed that poverty could be abolished by economic growth supported by a welfare 'first aid' service. The imbalance which produced pockets of poverty in an otherwise affluent society must be rectified not only by fiscal redistribution but by regulating the economies of both the public and private sectors. Modern society with its increasing range of consumer choices (many of them unrelated to real demands) neglected the public sector, to the detriment of the 'minority poor' (the old, ethnic minorities, etc.) who still relied on the public sector for basic services. A nation of car owners neglects public transport and falling standards hit the non-car owning pensioner. Excellent private medical care in the USA is often achieved at the expense of the public hospital service—the negro or the Puerto Rican suffers. Schools in middle-class areas cream off the best teachers so that the educational system in the twilight areas of the inner city is impoverished.

The situation first analysed by Galbraith and Harrington in the United States and later in Britain by Townsend, Abel-Smith and Titmuss is most significantly one in which poverty is not identified with a specific class. Politicians, it is true, will speak of the poor and underprivileged as 'the working class' but this association will not stand up to examination. For the first time in history our poor are now a minority group, forming what Martin Luther King called 'lonely islands of poverty in an ocean of material prosperity'. They are people who for one reason or another are missing out on the general benefit which 'people's capitalism' affords the majority. Politically they are unrelated to each other and are not truly represented by any one political party or ideology. Luther King cherished the possibility of an alliance between the negro and the low-paid white worker, but it remains to be realized in concrete political terms. The elderly and the mentally sick are scandalously hard done by in Britain today, but there is little or no chance that they will become effective political allies.

Another feature of present-day poverty in developed societies is the difficulty of enabling underprivileged groups to achieve political expression. Some of the areas of suffering discussed in this book are beginning to be stirred to self-help of a kind. The family squatters movement is an example. The Disablement Income Group is another. But for many of the groups studied here, champions have had to come from outside the ranks of the oppressed. Fortunately it can be said that with very few exceptions those who do elect to give political voice to today's poor are unselfconsciously throwing in their lot with the victims. Lady Bountifuls who enjoy 'slumming' are mercifully on the decline.

The 'minority poor' are assailed time and again by the jibe that by the standards of the Indian peasant an unemployed Glaswegian in a Gorbals 'single end' or an old age pensioner in Notting Hill is a millionaire. In New York, journalists have told Puerto Rican immigrants in the slums of East Harlem to measure themselves against the standards of their kinsmen in the Caribbean. This argument totally ignores the social psychology of poverty, especially the psychology of minority poverty. It was some years after I had visited the Gorbals that I read the famous tale of pre-war Glasgow, *No Mean City*.[4] What struck me most was a sense of the relative well-being of the pre-war Gorbals. It was, as it remained in the 1960s, dirty, noisy, verminous and violent. But in the 1930s there was a sense of working-class solidarity which certainly contributed to the creation of the pre-war 'Red' Clydeside. By the time I knew the Gorbals it had become a kind of ghetto, a community compounded of socially inadequate families and families who were slowly moving down the adequacy scale. The poverty of the Gorbals did not help to identify its inhabitants with the rest of working-class Britain as it had done forty years ago; instead it branded them as social outcasts. As Galbraith puts it: 'People are poverty-stricken when their income, even if it is adequate for survival, falls markedly below that of the community. Then they cannot have what the larger community regards as the minimum necessary for decency; and they cannot wholly escape, therefore, the judgement of the larger community that they are indecent.'[5]

An encouraging feature of the 'rediscovery' of poverty in the last decade is the emergence of new forms of community action which are significantly different from both old-style voluntary work and from traditional politics. The 1960s in Britain was the era of the pressure group, when pragmatic radicals banded together to champion specific groups within society and to achieve certain specific but limited results. Most of the original and vital anti-poverty activity has been performed by groups like Shelter, DIG, the Child Poverty Action Group, Age Concern and the Simon Community. Most of the contributors to this symposium are active within one or other of these organizations. On the whole we tend to be young and radical but not doctrinaire. Far too many of us, I believe in retrospect, live and work in London. We do not aim to provide clear-cut solutions to the problems of poverty and under-privilege about which we write, but we do hope that our observations will not only shape social thinking in the political parties but cause all readers to reflect on the desirability of far-reaching change in society. Perhaps the greatest hope for the latter is to be found in the many community development projects which are getting under way in various urban areas. One such development which deserves sympathetic consideration is the newly-founded Committee for City Poverty of which Lord Harlech, National Chairman of Shelter, is the President.

It is not our intention in this survey of current social evils to give the impression that nothing has been done, or can be done, about them. There are various excellent bodies, in addition to the new pressure groups we represent, who have been trying for many years —with some success—to ameliorate conditions in all the fields we cover: homelessness, physical and mental disability, neglect of the old, educational and social casualty (both vagrancy and drug addiction), racism and poverty. Whether these bodies go far enough, or are tackling the problems in a truly effective manner, is open to question. Our object is to examine shortcomings frankly, some may think unfairly. To quote Bernard Shaw: 'The reasonable man adapts himself to the world; the unreasonable man persists in trying to adapt the world to himself. Therefore, all progress depends on the unreasonable man.'

We therefore, in this survey of current poverty, are pleased to take on the mantle of the unreasonable man.

IAN HENDERSON

NOTES

1 In Rowntree and Lavers, *Poverty and the Welfare State* (Longman, 1951). The two previous studies were: B. S. Rowntree, *Poverty: A Study of Town Life* (Macmillan, 1901), and B. S. Rowntree, *Poverty and Progress* (Longman, 1941).

2 K. Coates and R. Silburn, *Poverty: The Forgotten Englishmen* (Penguin, 1970).

3 J. K. Galbraith, *The Affluent Society* (Hamish Hamilton, 1958).

4 MacArthur and Long, *No Mean City* (Longman, 1935).

5 Galbraith, *op. cit.*, p. 252.

JOHN DOWNING

Equal Opportunity for Inequality: _Racism_ and Poverty in Britain

'Integration means "equal opportunity accompanied by cultural diversity, in an atmosphere of mutual tolerance" '—Roy Jenkins.

'The politician at the (national) level is usually more skilled than the politician at the local level, and when he wants to practise racism, he's more skilled in the practice of it than those who practise it at the local level'—Malcolm X.[1]

I

For many people, starvation is the essential poverty-line. While it is only proper therefore to assure people sufficient income to stay alive, nothing beyond that point belongs to them as of right. What they secure over and above life itself must be battled for.

This is a succinct statement of society's responsibility for its poor members as defined in some cultures (including British culture). It lies behind the claim that poverty has almost vanished in modern affluent Britain—for who starves to death or dies of exposure these days?

There is though one lurking difficulty in this argument which, when fully examined, uproots this view of poverty and demonstrates that in reality it is arbitrary and dangerous. From the simplest standpoint, the difficulty consists in the changing of standards with the passing of time. An obvious instance would be the quantity and quality of nutrition judged essential for survival. Many people in today's world live, and continue to live, _below_ what medical experts in Britain would consider to be the starvation-line for British people (in quantity, let alone quality). Similarly, the light, warmth and heat considered normal and taken for granted in present-day England would have been beyond imagining even two hundred years ago. So the definition of 'normal conditions' (and consequently of poverty) always emerges from what is normal for most people in a given society at a given time.

From another and much more decisive angle the lurking difficulty in this 'absolute' definition of poverty is the extraordinary assumption that humans only deserve to be kept alive, and that after this their rights cease. Perhaps the most tenacious theories are those which are allowed to remain unquestioned, but the tenacity of this one is certainly no measure of its merit when examined in the clear light of day. It plainly underwrites the harshest exploitation, since everything short of extortion by starvation is in principle admissible by one individual or class against another.

In this extreme form, many would reject the theory; but it persists in an inverted form which is powerful in shaping tolerance of inequality. Take for instance the common attitude in Britain to council housing with garages for workers. Either the policy is felt to be slightly improper, or it is taken as an index of the workers' having attained an astonishing degree of equality. The implication of the first view is that they do not deserve cars; of the second, that they need nothing else. But once it is realized that all humans have unqualified right to the fullest and richest life possible, given the state of development of productive forces, and *not* just to existence, then poverty has a very different profile from that conventionally drawn by conservatives *or radicals*. The essential fallacy lies in assessing poverty without reference to the degree of development of the forces of production. Such an omission leads either to the assertion that there is no poverty because everyone is better off than those somewhere else in the world, or at some other period in human history; or to the (radical) view that poverty still does exist, but only among certain specific minorities (the elderly, children of large families, and so on).

Against these distortions and confusions, it is essential to hold to the only objective criterion by which the profile of poverty can be drawn: the extent of social wealth in the here and now, and the way it is divided up. No one sensibly concerns themselves about the absolute obliteration of every last differentiation in human society, for that kind of pettifogging utopianism only acts as an excuse for avoiding the real issues about the *extremes* between wealth and poverty which currently exist in Britain and the world. It is the principal contradiction between the extraordinary development of productive forces and the extreme inequality with which they are enjoyed, that has to be the focus of thinking about poverty.

2

The measurement of these extremes is often answered (especially for Britain) in terms of income. This trivializes the whole issue. A scientific analysis must include (a) total wealth, economic insecurity, exposure to ill health, and the question of *power*; (b) the explanation for these extremes, in which power and powerlessness are essential elements. This analysis will now be sketched. The bulk of the chapter will then investigate the specific place of black and brown migrant workers and their children in the current British profile of poverty, with attention drawn again to the reasons for their position and to those factors which make their experience different from the experience of white workers. (The fact that poverty is not the property merely of marginal minorities should not lead anyone to see the poor as one undifferentiated lump.)

Wealth has tended to be the focus of most writing about poverty, and is of course fundamental in one way or another to most or all of the dimensions of inequality. Why it is misleading to assess wealth in terms of 'take home pay' is important on two grounds. First, at the upper end of the scale there are many forms of wealth such as company cars and houses not represented in 'take home pay'.[2] Second, at the other end of the scale expenditure problems are often much greater. The hoary example is a large family with a small income, but two others are equally important. Having to buy an item through hire-purchase because you cannot pay cash means paying perhaps 30 per cent more for it. The cost of accommodation may be disproportionate: in 1968, precisely the lowest quarter of London households, earning *under* £20 a week, had to pay 28 per cent of this for shelter—the accommodation in question cannot often be described as a 'home' in the accepted sense.[3] All the evidence available renders the extreme inequalities of wealth in Britain beyond dispute. Nor is the Welfare State the great leveller-up it has been falsely claimed to be.[4]

Economic security obviously hinges on wealth, but is such a dominant part of the life-experience of the poor that it is worth discussing in its own right. Insecurity is the characteristic quality of the relation between employer and employee in a capitalist economy. The extent of this insecurity varies, and for a long time the greater security attached to many white-collar jobs was quite an important reason for white-collar workers to hold themselves aloof from militant blue-collar union struggles. More recently, with computerized office-work and other innovations, office clerks and even insurance- and bank-clerks have come to appreciate how much insecurity they have in common with manual workers. Middle management in Britain has been experiencing the same cold winds since the late 1960s. Craft unionism has always been another defence against insecurity; but fast technical change is repeatedly used by employers to destroy crafts, and so their owners' strength as employees. The reverse tactic, from the confidential clerk to the whizzkid technical expert, has generally been to do everything possible to 'attach' workers currently thought essential, and to make them *feel* part of the operation.[5]

Health has always been much better among the wealthy than among the poor. An unskilled worker's family, for instance, is $2\frac{1}{2}$ times more likely to experience the tragedy of infant mortality than is an upper-class family. Nor is poor health only due to bad housing, poor sanitation, chronic damp, and overcrowding, though all of these take their toll of the poor. Manual work, never the province of the wealthy, is quite dangerous. For instance, from 1960–68 the construction industry has claimed on average 254 deaths a year *at work*; factories averaged 353 deaths a year over the same period. And in 1968 alone, non-fatal accidents at work exceeded 260,000.[6] Illness shows a similar picture; the semi-skilled and unskilled suffer much higher rates of pneumonia, bronchitis, stomach-complaints, arthritis and rheumatism than the rest of the population. Pneumonia and bronchitis are much more likely to kill in these social categories, too. Disease, especially TB, follows the same lines. . . . Lastly, the myth that mental illness is especially a luxury of the upper classes is demolished by the available evidence. Schizophrenia in particular increases in incidence as you travel down the social scale.[7]

Power is the kind of topic on which the conventional wisdom generally has difficulty in restraining itself. The universal franchise, together with the sinister stranglehold of the unions, is felt to guarantee far more power to the lower layers of English society than to the upper layers (and probably far more than is good for them). Where is power, though, in casting one vote every five years for a person you have not selected, who will almost certainly belong to a party indistinguishable in most respects from the others, and who also has a very slim chance of a decision-making post in the Cabinet? Moreover in 75 per cent of the seats at any British general election, the outcome is so certain that vote-casting is a mere formality.[8]

As regards the unions' stranglehold, it is worth noting that they only have their hands around the throats of less than half of the labour-force. The rest, including most of the lowest paid, are not unionized. Even the strength they have has been savaged by the 1971 Industrial Relations Act, which instituted State control over union rules, banned sympathy strikes, and established a host of other repressive measures to cut the sinews of workers' self-defence. Nor should the *actual* militance of British unions, as distinct from their purely verbal militance, be overestimated when assessing their effectiveness on behalf of the poor.[9]

Conversely, the power of multi-product and multi-national corporations, of the banks, of the insurance companies, and of major finance companies, is gigantic. It is hard to measure with precision, since so much of this power operates in relative secrecy. Such 'discretion' has the effect of removing this whole sphere of modern society from the forefront of many people's minds. It also makes it easy for the apologists of these institutions to allay any half-thought-out fears about their immense power. It is hard to argue when the facts are so hard to come by. But anyone can recognize the power that major industrial and financial institutions must wield, even though not everyone is aware of the full implications of the lack of control the man-in-the-street and even the shareholder-in-the-street have over their operations.[10] For the moment let the last word lie with Lord Beeching, who candidly confesses that his search for power drove him away from politics into the locus of real power, the vast modern corporations.[11] Power indeed.

In general, it seems that the little power the poor have in the present structure of society is the power to veto from time to time. But the positive power to initiate and carry through a programme of action is never theirs. And it is this power alone which is really worth having, for it alone is capable of finally conquering poverty.

The prospect for leaving poverty behind is therefore one of its crucial aspects. There are two possible roads, of which the first, best and most difficult is what might be called 'collective upward mobility' out of poverty. In other words, the poor as a whole improve their position by moving as a bloc. The obvious merit of this revolutionary change is that the condition is abolished (which in practice means that starvation and extremes *both* disappear, as noted).

The second, less attractive possibility is that individuals may struggle their way out of poverty. Those who do are often those with talents which would be valuable in leading collective upward mobility. Not only then may their success rob the poor of leadership, but it can also be utilized as evidence for the willingness of the present ruling class to welcome collective upward mobility—the implication being that the only factor blocking it is lack of motivation by the poor!

In actuality, the present British social structure is profoundly geared to inequality. Mass free education, for instance, often viewed as the Great Relocator of talent from all strata, has been shown by quantities of research to be far more likely to maintain children in their parents' status than to change it. *Not only is it inefficient*, its precise aim, its whole organization, is to feed broad sections of the labour-market, from highly-paid research scientists to low-paid shop assistants. Its essence is to service a colossally unequal occupational work structure.[12] Opportunities for individuals to make good are also irrelevant to the continuing problem of poverty and inequality, unless those individuals refuse to allow their success to deflect them from the commitment to struggle against poverty and inequality by any means necessary.

3

This is a good point at which to draw together the threads so far. Clearly wealth and health and economic security and power (or their absence) are all closely interrelated; but if we are to move beyond a fuller *description* of poverty than 'take home pay', it is now necessary to explain the origin of poverty.[13] In so doing, it is |

important to emphasize once again that the definition of poverty does not consist of some arbitrary minimum (of wealth, power, or anything else), but is fixed by the maximum attainable at a particular stage of development; and that the poor therefore are far more in number than just the elderly, the black, the disabled, and other minorities. They consist of something like the bottom nine-tenths of British society, who between them all, own only 17 per cent of the total personal wealth in Britain (the top tenth enjoys the other 83 per cent). By world standards, to label almost anyone in Britain 'poor' is of course grotesque; but in terms of ending world poverty, the recognition of British poverty is very significant. For until the British poor overcome the inequalities internal to Britain, it is extremely doubtful that they will be able to recast their actions against international poverty.

For both British inequalities and global inequalities are products of the world capitalist order—or more precisely, of world anarchy generated by the processes of capitalist 'development'.[14] To demonstrate this contention to the unwilling is beyond the scope of this chapter;[15] but let me trace out the simplest basic causal connections between capitalism as a form of economic organization, and British poverty.

The most straightforward way of approaching the matter is to ask a series of questions. Is it *accidental* that in Britain such colossal quantities of wealth are concentrated in so few hands? Is it an *oversight* that the farther down the social scale you go, the greater your economic insecurity? Does the British ruling class not really *realize* that risk of illness and accident increases the farther you pass from their happy lot? And does that dominant class systematically *encourage* (by education and media) the mass of the population to share much more equally in their wealth, so leaving poverty behind for good?

The obvious answer, unless quite exceptional stupidity of various kinds is to be credited to the dominant forces in British society, is to each question 'no'. *The essential reason is that the motor of capitalism is the control of investment by sectional minorities who need not be accountable to the producers, rather than control by representatives of the producers who would be subject to instant recall* (socialism). On this foundation, in any society, all kinds of laws and institutions and world-views emerge and develop that tend to have the general effect of underpinning the *status quo* (sometimes by the subtle means of altering its contours without changing its core).

This being so, sharp variations in wealth, power, health, safety, and economic security, must take at best second place to the basic dynamic of capitalism. In principle, with that extraordinary concentration of power, a capitalist class might be thought to have a unique ability to end poverty, to change this dynamic to a different set of priorities. Were it to do so, capitalism in that context would cease; but there is no record of any such class ever showing the faintest inclination to abolish itself. It is frankly romantic to visualize such an about-face actually taking place. Therefore control and ownership of most wealth by a sectional and unaccountable minority is the fundamental social fact at the root of poverty.

The dominance of this sectional minority is kept in being by a whole arsenal of weapons, from many laws and the legal apparatus (courts, police, prisons) at the 'blunt' end, through to confused and confusing analysis and communication of the realities of social life (in party politics, education, and the media) at the 'gentle' end. This interrelated arsenal has grown up over years and even centuries, with its own varying emphases and styles, *without* any direction from a top-hatted knot of greedy conspirators—though here again, the processes can't be traced out now.

The only solution to the perpetual problem of poverty is therefore the construction of a new economic *order* by the masses of the poor. Only so can collective upward mobility, the abolition of poverty, be achieved. We return inexorably to the question of power and powerlessness, and of why in a liberal democracy like Britain the poor have not achieved this after about two centuries of intermittent agitation against the impact on them of capitalist economic organization. If the poor are powerless, why are they?

In concrete British terms, over and above questions about the 'arsenal' sketched a moment ago, this implies questions such as the following. Whose interests did the Labour Party represent when it tried (1969) to introduce laws to *weaken* the self-defence organizations of the poor (i.e. its Industrial Relations Bill) or when after six years in office it left inequality about where it had been?[16] Whose interests does the leadership of a number of trade unions represent when it is prepared to co-operate with 'incomes policies' designed to control the rate at which the poor can struggle to increase their share of wealth? Or when it accepts over its members' heads derisory pay increases rendered null and void in advance by price-inflation? And whose interests do the minor warring leftist sectarians represent as they vie with each other as to which is the purest Marxist-Leninist of them all?

Is it not the case then that the fundamental precondition for successful struggle for power by the poor, i.e. a mass revolutionary party, is scarcely on the horizon, and that consequently there is no end in sight to poverty in Britain? No such party; no consciousness of the real issues; reliance on the Labour Party and current trade-union leadership 'as all there is'; no desire or determination in those quarters to grasp the nettles; cynicism about the opportunities for vital social change : poverty grinds on, apparently some kind of law of human nature.

4

So far the focus has been on what poverty is, why it is, and the chances of ending it in Britain. The question to be answered now is the relation of about 1½ million black and brown migrant workers and their children, now a sector of British society, to the other sectors of that society.

Should anyone be in any doubt that black people in Britain are overwhelmingly concentrated at the poorest end of the society, the data from the 1961 Census, the 1966 Sample Census and no doubt the 1971 Census reveal the tiny proportions in white-collar work, and the vast majority that is in semi-skilled and unskilled work.[17] This means low wages; and the very high proportion of women at work, especially in the Caribbean community, not only points to the low earnings of their men, but also involves them in being grossly underpaid simply as women workers.[18] Furthermore, the general unemployment is hitting black workers extremely hard, most especially black school-leavers.[19]

Further, as previously noted, *wealth* is determined by the inroads made on it. Dependents (often in the country of origin too) represent one important demand on the earnings of migrant workers.[20] Another particularly severe burden is the question of housing, since the price black people have to pay for it is well known to be higher (even though the accommodation is generally worse) than white people have to pay. A study in Lambeth in 1966, for instance, showed the average white weekly rent was £3.60, the average black rent £4.25. The high proportion of black tenants in furnished accommodation also suffers from higher than average rents. Further, those black people who have obtained mortgages in the private sector very often have to pay higher interest-rates over a shorter term than do whites. One index of the hardship that results is the extent to which black people are forced to share accommodation : 70 per cent in London (as against 31 per cent for whites) and 40 per cent in the West Midlands (as against 4 per cent for whites).[21]

As regards *economic insecurity*, black migrant workers are subject to all the hazards usual in that sector of society, together with certain additional ones. Again, housing is a major question. Some local authorities refuse to rehouse them properly or according to need.[22] Given the lesser degree of security in furnished tenancies, the fact that 44 per cent of black tenants rent furnished rooms in London and 21 per cent in the West Midlands (as against 3 per cent and 2 per cent of whites) is significant.[23] A final disadvantage of furnished tenancies is that some local authorities will not, or are reluctant to, rehouse from them.[24] It is known now too that a very large section of the rapidly growing homeless in London are black, despite the fact that only 10 per cent are in rent arrears, and only 8 per cent are unemployed (far lower rates than among white homeless families).[25]

On the question of *health*, it is worth adding that over and above the 'usual' risks, there are some indications that rates of schizophrenia are higher than would be expected. This is *not* the result of 'culture clash', but a response to the hostility and strains experienced living in a racist society.[26]

On *power* and powerlessness, the identical story repeats itself, with certain particularly destructive forms of repression added. In this context it is necessary to discuss the political system, the legal system, and system of local authority services.

It is abundantly clear that in the national political system black people are only an issue.[27] They emerge only as the objects of the major parties' efforts to outdo each other in proposals to stop them entering Britain. Even a measure such as the 1968 Race Relations Act, publicly presented as geared to their needs, had little or nothing to do with them—which no doubt helps to explain its feeble enforcement procedures. It was piloted through Parliament as a result of three forces : skilful lobbying by upper middle-class whites; the Labour Cabinet's desire to appease the liberal-radical wing of the parliamentary party for racist immigration legislation (of which the Kenyan Asians' measure was only the nadir); and the presence of a favourably inclined Home Secretary (Jenkins) at a particular juncture. No power to the people here !

Similarly, in 1968 the Labour Government refused—at a time when the matter was under review with the passage of the Race Relations Bill—to contemplate making the present Community Relations Commission into a National Council for Racial Equality to act as a vehicle to articulate black people's interests, with executive members largely elected from a constituency of black organizations.[28] This refusal was the response of men who could not care less about the future of the black community in British society, so long as the whites could be kept tolerably electorally cheerful.

Despite possible appearances to the contrary therefore, black migrant workers and their families and children have no levers on power. The chances are negligible in our corrupt version of democracy that a *poor* minority will have the right to be listened to. With a wealthy minority (industrialists, City businessmen) the situation is of course reversed. Occasionally in a black area, where an electoral candidate may be unsure of his seat, black people may see a glimmering of power, since the candidate may decide to recognize their existence if he needs to court their vote. But what kind of real control does that give them over their lives?

As well as the general class bias of the legal system—low availability of lawyers in poor neighbourhoods, the patchy working of the legal aid provisions, the absence of legal aid for key tribunals (rent, social security), the colossal pressure on the minority of anti-privilege lawyers—there is a whole range of other factors which are used in a specially repressive manner against blacks.

The one which has received the most publicity, is probably police violence against black people. As always, the police are not generally so stupid as to commit their violence, or even to be especially offensive, in front of neutral observers with cameras. But commit it they frequently do;[29] and the offences tend to concentrate on a number of stations in particular. Instances in London include the Harrow Road, Ladywell and Brixton stations. Recently a massive

whitewash operation has been mounted, with local police community relations specialists being appointed, and impeccably liberal
sentiments being expressed by senior police officials. The harass-
ment and assaults experienced by black people from the police still
continue.

In these activities policemen enjoy an important source of
support from some magistrates, who are often willing (even en-
thusiastic) supporters of the police version of an incident, however
implausible. Even in those cases where the police account of an
event would be laughable if it were not directed against an actual
person, JPs may dismiss the case, but without any statement which
would assist the black defendant in filing a suit for wrongful arrest,
assault, etc. And at the prison end of the legal system, the life of
the black prisoner can be in very serious danger.[30]

The system of local authority services is rightly coming under
increasing attack for the hardships it creates for the people it is
officially designed to help.[31] It is obviously further the case that
Asian migrant workers are under an extra (linguistic) disability in so
far as local councils do not bother to create interpreting services. In
general, there is the double problem once again : local authority
services are not designed to end, but to smooth over the problems
poor people face;[32] in addition the officials who man these services
are averagely imbued with the racism traditional in British culture.
The account of the housing visitors in Burney's book is just one
case in point.[33]

Powerlessness in the face of the State is then something which
begins for black migrant workers from the moment they enter the
country,[34] and continues from there on. It is to be wondered therefore what a leading politician (Wilson) had in mind when in a
speech on race relations in Birmingham in 1968, which had been
billed as an *answer* to Powell, he spoke of 'the sinister development
of black power'. So much for realism, or justice.

The clutches of poverty are therefore for no sector of British
society more tenacious than for black migrant workers. On top of
all the other problems faced by a white worker in trying to escape
from poverty, there is the further barrier of racial discrimination.
Every white person who discriminates is in effect policing the
superior social position of the white majority; so that black workers
find themselves facing not merely the top 10 per cent, and the State,

but a substantial proportion of the white majority as well. As well as affecting individual mobility out of poverty, this has a drastic impact on the chances of collective upward mobility for black and white alike. To the degree that blacks and whites see the principal contradiction in society as existing between themselves, and not as between themselves on the one hand and the controllers of wealth and power on the other, so much the farther away is an end to their jointly experienced poverty and powerlessness.

The reasons why whites are racist, and the reason why black workers have migrated to Britain, are both founded (once again) on the capitalist economic organization of British and world society. How?

Taking the second point first, it is clear from a comparative overview of labour migration in Europe since 1945[35] that as each Western European economy expanded so it demanded more and more workers from overseas to fill its least popular jobs. In France, Algerians and Portuguese; in the German Federal Republic, Italians, Spaniards, Turks, Yugoslavs and even (South) Koreans; in Switzerland, Italians; in Holland, West Indians, Moroccans, Indonesians, Spaniards; in Britain, West Indians, Asians, Irish, and others. In none of these societies save the Netherlands (and there in an incomplete and rather destructively 'assimilationist' manner) has any proper provision been made for these migrant workers and their dependents in terms of 'infrastructure' (i.e. housing, schools, transport, medical and social services). The pull of the labour market across frontiers and oceans, coupled with unconcern for the social rights of migrant workers, is the kind of utilization/exploitation of labour classically characteristic of capitalism. Capital's demand for their labour is why they have come, and why they are concentrated among the poorest workers : that is where capital wanted them.

The reasons why white workers discriminate against black workers are also to be discovered in the nature of capitalist 'development'. The racist justifications for imperialism and slavery,[36] that ingrained fear and contempt of black people in English cultural traditions, have been in turn transmitted through literature, school textbooks, music-halls, and other means. Then, too, there is no significant agency in British society that has encouraged whites to see blacks either as worthy of the same respect, or indeed as anything but improper competitors for scarce (infrastructural) resources—housing,

B

schooling, jobs, services.[37] Finally, the accumulation of new barriers to the entry of black migrants from 1962–71, followed by Powell's speeches, have acted to extend and rigidify white racism. This political 'contribution' consists precisely of a totally false 'solution' to the hardships created by clustering jobs and so workers in the Midlands and the South East, *without* the corresponding infrastructure. It is typical of a corrupt capitalist 'democracy' to permit white and black workers to be starved of resources, and then to argue (via immigration laws, and so on) that without black migrant workers such hardship will not occur in future, or would not have occurred in the first place!

The ancestry of poverty, labour migration and racism is traceable then in each case to the capitalist organization of British and world society. Because of the third factor, the black experience of British institutions is objectively and intensively worse than white workers' experience of them. The connivance of many whites in this last situation, ranging from tolerance of it to membership of fascist groups, gives black workers every discouragement to join in any economic struggles over wages and rents, let alone any struggle for political power. Because whites often experience a somewhat better deal, they can convince themselves they are significantly more 'in', socially and economically, than blacks, and thus that they are no longer on the very bottom, and so have one more reason[38] for discounting the need for political (or *sharp* economic) class struggle. No one in the capitalist class could hope for a better Christmas gift —except that like most other social relations, racism is double-edged.

The experience of the struggle for black liberation in the United States and against the US aggression and genocidal attacks in South East Asia, has served to awaken many whites to the realities of life.[39] No regime has so perfected racist oppression to date that it does not arouse increasing opposition among the majority, which in turn overflows on to the way the entire society is organized. Similarly in Britain, the growing voice of black protest, and the repression in the north of Ireland, is beginning to awaken many people to what Britain is, and to the stifling of their own rights and potential. Naturally, a quietist attitude will not see the transition from these early beginnings to a mass movement against poverty and racism, and for a new economic, political and social order: anyone committed to these ends has massive tasks ahead. But nor is it the case that the dominant forces of power and wealth hold all the cards, even when they seem to. (I shall return to this topic at the end of the chapter.)

5

I intend to conclude the chapter with some observations on certain specific aspects of the situation of the black migrant worker which make it clumsy and inaccurate simply to claim that he is oppressed 'like anyone else'. One of the most significant points is the experience of racial discrimination, which has been repeatedly analysed already. This does not mean the analysis has been in any sense complete; and in order that it should not seem dangerously incomplete, there are two further dimensions of it that must be noted.

Firstly there is the permanence of skin-colour as a distinguishing signal. Jan Ludwig Hoch can become Robert Maxwell, millionaire publisher MP with an upper-class accent; Gunter Kees can become William Davis, editor of *Punch*; and people have to be *told* their origins. But never so with black people. Secondly there is the highly destructive effect on the self-concept and identity-formation of the children of black migrant workers, of participating in the institutions of a racist society (notably its schools); assimilation is if anything even more dangerous than discrimination.[40]

One of the most popular forms of blurring the fact of racism is to treat black people as a problem. The writer recalls seeing a *Panorama* programme divided equally between a documentary and discussion of venereal disease, and a documentary and discussion of black immigration, which was concluded by Robin Day noting that these were two major social problems, and he would be seeing us next week. The use of the term 'colour problem' or 'race problem' normally implies (a) that black people are responsible for it through having the temerity to come here in the first place (the very term, *colour* problem, implies the exoneration of the English, who are rarely labelled as coloured); (b) that black migrant workers are to be lumped together with VD, drugs, prostitution, violent crime, and other 'problems'; and (c) that black people are therefore a real nuisance, because who wants another bloody social problem?

The term 'problem' may also imply for some other people that a little deft social engineering, a couple of strips of social elastoplast, will put Humpty together again. So black people become the special exotic province of those who would like to try their hand at a little bit of social reform and experimentation—so long as they can plan it from their leafy gardens.

The last perspective has led to a peculiar disadvantage for black migrant workers in Britain. They have been subjected to a whole industry that has grown up about *but not for* them. There is the Community Relations Commission, founded on a series of myths about the nature of community[41] which can always be relied upon to squelch any vigorous initiative from any of its local committees or officers which challenges Establishment racism. There is the Race Relations Board, which has neither the teeth nor the inclination to make any impact against racial injustice.[42] There is the Runnymede Trust, dominated by big business and ex-colonials,[43] which specializes in telling the Press that Powell's sums are wrong (who cares if they're right?). There is the £40,000 a year Bristol University 'Research Unit on Ethnic Relations', founded by the Social Science Research Council, which will in time produce its heaps of trivia on those zoo-inhabitants who have consented to talk to it. For a long time there was the Institute of Race Relations which in 1969 as a major fruit of its endeavours published a massive dialogue addressed to the Home Office *about* black people which it brandished as a (scientific) Survey of Race Relations in Great Britain.[44] All these bodies, along with the Home Office Advisory Committee on Race Relations, the Minority Rights Group, the nearly defunct Africa Bureau, have interlocking directorates or 'race relations experts' combined with major business interests (though in 1972 the Institute of Race Relations broke out of this pattern).

The absurd end-result has been however that blacks are worse off than they would have been without these agencies, yet many whites are convinced that if you are black you get specially favoured treatment with powerful friends on high—the worst of all possible worlds!

A comparison which many people have been strongly drawn to is that of the oppression of women and the oppression of black people. While certainly not denying the oppression of women, and while black women at work suffer particularly because of low female pay, *equating* sexual and racial oppression is ridiculous.

Women are scattered through all strata of society, and share in their husbands' wealth, status, and so on. They are not concentrated at the bottom as are black people.

Further, it is very necessary to recognize that neither women as such, nor widows, nor the disabled present an electoral advantage or personal gain to anyone who cares to attack them openly. Shocking apathy in the face of their plight, together with subtle and pervasive sexism, there certainly is; but there is no Enoch Powell dedicated to an active campaign against their interests and gaining popularity by doing so.

To conclude : the major emphasis of this chapter has tended to be on black people as objects of other people's actions. *Although this is fundamentally one-sided*, since obviously black people have a life of their own despite this and are not waiting to be brought to life by white acceptance, I do not feel inclined to redress the balance. This is mostly because the British ruling class is repressive enough without directing its attention any further toward (for instance) black self-defence and political groups; and also partly because I think if this dimension is written about it would be done much better by a committed black writer or writers.

On the other hand, there is one aspect of the self-assertion of black people which it is both safe and essential to write about. In so doing I intend to take up again the question of how far the dominant forces in Britain and the world have the situation sewn up (see the end of section 4); and also the statement of Roy Jenkins about integration at the head of this chapter. The self-assertion to which I refer is of course the revolution in the dependent areas of the world (Asia, Africa, Latin America) against colonialism and neo-imperialism. The colonial yoke has largely been shattered; the neo-imperial yoke remains.[45]

As fragments of the Third World, most migrant workers in Britain increasingly take pride and heart in the extraordinary achievements of the Chinese, Vietnamese and Cuban peoples, not forgetting the struggle of African Americans inside the USA itself. These achievements naturally call into question and threaten the racist and imperialist international domination of the West, with dangerous implications for the survival of capitalism as the world economic system. Although it will take *internal* struggle and conflict in North America, Western Europe and Japan finally to move toward a new economic, political and social order, in conjunction with liberation struggles in the Third World, these developments constitute the furthest advance yet toward the eradication of racism. It is therefore emphatically *not* the case that black migrant workers and their families in Britain are 'alone in the world', or that their allies in the Third World are condemned to offering merely moral support. With every victory against the imperialist structure of capitalist production, the economic system that engendered European racism and that fosters it within the West today moves nearer to its end. That is much more than moral support.

It is for this reason that Roy Jenkins's definition of integration ('equal opportunity—cultural diversity—mutual tolerance') is distorting. Not because mutual tolerance between people of different national origins is undesirable, nor yet because opportunity should be unequal! But his pluralist nirvana takes no account of the realities of its context; no account of the inequality at the core of British and world society for which he wishes there to be equal opportunity; no account of the extent to which cultural diversity is used as one means of maintaining inequality between black and white and white and white in British society! After this, what room is there for an atmosphere of mutual tolerance—a calmly unequal Britain, set moreover as jewel in a silver sea apparently insulated from the network of imperialist domination of the world? The only context in which this definition would not be distorting would be in a just socialist society. Neither Roy Jenkins nor his party (let alone any other major political party in Britain), will ever bring about such a society because of their consistent refusal to grasp the giant nettles involved. The especially oppressed position of black people in Britain, together with the exploitation and oppression of the majority of British people, will not be done away with by this definition of 'integration' or the intentions it expresses. The recognition of this truth is a necessary step towards the abolition of that oppression and exploitation in Britain.

> Right now our disease must be identified as capitalist man and his monstrous machine, a machine with the senseless and calloused ability to inflict these wounds programmed into its every cycle. . . . It has robbed me of these twenty eight years. It has robbed us all for nearly half a millennium. The greatest bandit

of all time, we'll stop him now. . . . It's very contradictory for a man to teach about the murder in corporate capitalism, to isolate and expose the murderers behind it, to instruct that these madmen are completely without stops, are licentious, totally depraved —and then not make adequate preparations to defend himself from the madman's attack.[46]

. . . if you want to know what his language is, study his history. His language is blood, his language is power, his language is brutality, his language is everything that's brutal. . . . But don't let anyone who's oppressing us ever lay the ground rules. Don't go by their game, don't play the game by their rules. Let them know that this is a new game, and we've got some new rules, and these rules mean anything goes, *anything goes.*[47]

NOTES

1 Malcolm X, *By Any Means Necessary* (New York: Pathfinder Press, 1970), p. 164.

2 For extended discussions see R. M. Titmuss, *Income Distribution and Social Change* (Allen & Unwin, 1962); J. E. Meade, *Efficiency, Equality and the Ownership of Property* (Allen & Unwin, 1964); K. Coates and R. Silburn, *Poverty: The Forgotten Englishmen* (Penguin, 1970); M. Meacher, 'Wealth: Labour's Achilles' Heel', in P. Townsend and N. Bosanquet, *Labour and Inequality* (Fabian Society, 1972), ch. 11.

3 The overall average outgoing being 15.6 per cent of income. See Judy Hillman, *Planning for London* (Penguin Special, 1971), p. 58.

4 See the references in 2 above; also J. Kincaid's essay in N. Harris and J. Palmer, *World Crisis* (Hutchinson, 1971).

5 For clerkly work, see D. Lockwood, *The Blackcoated Worker* (Allen & Unwin, 1958). On 'attachment' see, for instance, the writings of the management theorist Douglas MacGregor; or the 1972 pamphlet on 'workers' *participation*' published by Aims of Industry, an unhesitatingly pro-capitalist body.

6 Annual Report of HM Chief Inspector of Factories 1968, Cmnd 4146 (HMSO, 1969).

7 W. P. D. Logan and A. A. Cushion, *Morbidity Statistics from General Practice,* vol. ii (General Register Office: Studies on Medical and Population Subjects 14, 1960), pp. 14, 16. E. Goldberg and S. Morrison, 'Schizophrenia and Social Class', in *British Journal of Psychiatry* 109 (1963), pp. 785–802.

8 J. Rasmussen, 'The Implications of Safe Seats for British Democracy', in R. Rose, *Policy-Making in Britain* (Macmillan, 1969), pp. 30–47.

9 See V. L. Allen, *The Sociology of Industrial Relations* (Longman, 1971), especially Part III; or from a centrist position, H. Pelling, *A History of British Trade Unionism* (Penguin, 1968).

10 See C. Levinson, *Capital, Inflation and the Multi-Nationals* (Allen & Unwin, 1971) for an analysis of the creation of inflation by large corporations, for instance.

11 Interview in London *Evening Standard*, 17 March, 1970.

12 E.g. J. W. B. Douglas, *The Home and the School* (Panther, 1968); D. Lawton, *Social Class, Language and Education* (Routledge & Kegan Paul, 1968); M. F. D. Young, *Knowledge and Control* (Collier-Macmillan, 1971); D. Cohen and M. Lazerson, 'Education and the Corporate Order' and J. Spring, 'Education and the Rise of the Corporate State', in *Socialist Revolution* 2, 2 (1972), pp. 47–101.

13 Something that a recent detailed exposé of the 1964–70 British Labour Government's abject failure to live up to its egalitarian myth entirely leaves out. I refer to *Labour and Inequality* (see 2 above) which engages in the most detailed analysis of poverty, with no real analysis of its origins. Hence the way is left clear for endless mini-proposals to end poverty for ever.

14 It is a perversion of the words 'order' and 'development' to apply them to the conditions of life of most living humans.

15 See e.g. M. Dobb, *Studies in the Development of Capitalism* (Routledge & Kegan Paul, 1963); P. Baran, *The Political Economy of Growth* (Penguin edition 1973); S. Amin, *L'Accumulation à l'Echelle Mondiale* (Paris: Anthropos, 2nd ed., 1971); C. Palloix, *L'Economie Mondiale Capitaliste* (Paris: Maspéro, 1972); C. R. Hensman, *Rich Against Poor* (Allen Lane, 1971); H. Magdoff, *The Age of Imperialism* (Monthly Review Press, 1968); P. Jalée, *The Third World in World Economy* (Monthly Review Press, 1969).

16 George Wigg's memoirs (*Sunday Times*, 23 April, 1972) throw ironic light on the warm relations between Callaghan (Chancellor 1964–67) and Lord Cromer, extreme right-wing Governor of the Bank of England, later Tory Government ambassador to Washington. Even more ironic is Jenkins's public image as campaigner against poverty (1972) and anti-racist. As Chancellor (1967–70) his budgets set in motion the present high unemployment; and he voted in Cabinet for every piece of racist immigration control passed by the Labour Government (e.g. the Kenyan Asians' measure of March 1968, which stopped British *passport-holders* of Asian origin entering Britain).

17 See E. J. B. Rose, *Colour and Citizenship* (OUP, 1969), tables 13.1/10. The book as a whole must be used with extreme caution: its size does not reflect the accuracy of its reasoning!

18 *Low Pay* (TUC General Council Discussion Document, 1970), Tables VII–XII. XVIII–XXII, drawn from the *New Earnings Survey* of the Department of Employment, September 1968.

19 Barbara Omar, 'Towards a Repatriation Bill?' *Race Today*, March 1972, pp. 93–4; also article by J. Lawless in *Business Management*, July 1970, pp. 27–31.

20 Overseas dependents may represent a 7–8 per cent demand on post-tax income. See another suspect book, K. Jones and A. D. Smith, *The Economic Impact of Commonwealth Immigration* (CUP, 1970), pp. 93–4.

21 See Table 12.3, p. 126; and pp. 190–3, 313–16, of *Colour and Citizenship* (see 17 above).

22 E. Burney, *Housing on Trial* (OUP, 1967); the Cullingworth Report, *Council Housing: Purposes, Procedures and Priorities* (HMSO, 1969), paras. 352–91.

23 Table 12.8, p. 133, *Colour and Citizenship* (see 17 above).

24 Cullingworth Report, Table 10, p. 81 (see 22 above).

25 J. Greve, *Homelessness in London* (Scottish Academic Press, 1971). Formerly a report to the Ministry of Housing, it became mysteriously 'lost', and was eventually published privately.

26 C. Bagley, 'Migration, Race and Mental Health', *Race*, IX, 3, January 1968; also his 'The Social Aetiology of Schizophrenia in Immigrant Groups', *Race Today*, October 1969.

27 See J. D. H. Downing, 'Racism in British Politics', in R. Mast and J. D. H. Downing, *Minority Demands: US–UK Responses* (OUP, forthcoming.

28 The 'Wood Proposals'—see Michael and Ann Dummett, 'The Role of the Government in Britain's Present Racial Crisis', in L. Donnelly, *Justice First* (Sheed & Ward, 1969), pp. 25–78.

29 See W. D. Wood and J. D. H. Downing, *Vicious Circle* (SPCK, 1968), pp. 22–3, 53–5; D. Humphrey and G. John, *Because They're Black* (Penguin, 1971), chs. 3, 12, 13; *Private Eye*, 213 (13 February, 1970), pp. 17–18; R. Phillips, 'The Death of One Lame Darkie', *Race Today*, January 1972, pp. 16–18; D. Humphrey and G. John, *Police Power and Black People* (Panther, 1972); and *Race Today*'s 'Area Round-Up' under the heading *Police*, monthly.

30 See 'Letter From Prison', *Race Today*, January 1971, pp. 22–4—it is very naïve to suppose that only US warders and prisoners are viciously racist.

31 T. Gould and J. Kenyon, *Voices from the Dole-Queue* (Temple-Smith, 1972); Rosalind Brooke, in *Labour and Inequality* (see 2 above); and *Poverty*, the Child Poverty Action Group's monthly.

32 Professor Greve sums up the role of social work (see 25), p. ix: 'The total contribution made by all these people is enormous. Without it London would be stricken by an avalanche of social problems of catastrophic proportions. Even relatively modest reductions in social service efforts in some fields . . . would quickly reveal deprivation and suffering . . . on a scale unimagined. . . . Adequate intelligence about . . . the problems and adequate resources to deal with them are essential. We are still a long way from fulfilling *either* of these basic requirements.' (My italics.)

33 *Housing on Trial* (see 22), pp. 72–7; G. Thomas, 'The Integration of Immigrants: A Note on the Views of Some Local Government Officials', *Race*, IX, 1, October 1967.

34 M. Dines, 'Immigration: The Tragic Obstacle Race', *Race Today*, March 1971; also her 'Repression: Immigration', *Ink*, 18 August, 1971; C. Chewaluza, 'No Entry', *RT*, June 1971; D. Humphrey, 'Pentonville: Prelude to Deportation', *RT*, May 1971; D. N. Sharma, 'Two Days at Heathrow', *RT*, July 1971; P. A. Agbarha, 'How To Be Deported', *RT*, August 1971; S. Genasci, 'The Home Office's Tangled Web', *RT*, September

1971; *Return to Sender* (Joint Council for the Welfare of Immigrants, September 1970).

35 S. Castles and G. Kosack, *Immigrant Workers and Class Structure in Western Europe* (OUP, 1973); also the articles by M. Nikolinakos and P. Cinnani in *Race Today*, November 1971.

36 V. G. Kiernan, *The Lords of Human Kind* (Penguin, 2nd ed., 1972); C. Bolt, *Victorian Attitudes to Race* (Routledge & Kegan Paul, 1971); W. D. Jordan, *White Over Black* (Penguin, 1971); Ann Dummett, *A Portrait of English Racism* (Penguin, 1973).

37 This is in no way to dishonour the individuals who have struggled against their institutions to attack racism. But neither the political parties, nor the educational and media system, nor the trade unions, nor the churches, have been noticeable *as such* for their anti-racist energies.

38 There are clearly many others, in education, the media, the advertizing barrage, the improvement on their parents' standard of living, the organizations of work, party politics, etc.

39 A development repeatedly stressed recently by Angela Davis, among others. See Angela Davis, *If they come in the morning . . .* (Orbach & Chambers, 1971), Part 2, 8.

40 See B. Coard, *How the West Indian Child is Made Educationally Subnormal in the English School System* (Beacon Books, 1971); also D. Milner, 'Prejudice and the Immigrant Child', *New Society*, 469, 23 September, 1971, pp. 556–9; and in general *The Autobiography of Malcolm X* (Penguin, 1969).

41 M. Hill and R. Issacharoff, *Community Action and Race Relations* (OUP, 1971).

42 See *Race Today*, October 1971, articles by Hetherington, Harrison, Goswami; and *RT*, November 1971, by Hetherington; also M. and A. Dummett, cited in 28 above, pp. 55–8.

43 See John Downing, 'Britain's race industry: harmony without injustice', *Race Today*, October 1972.

44 *Colour and Citizenship* (see 17 above). An abridged and superficially repainted version was published as N. Deakin, *Colour, Citizenship and British Society* (Panther, 1970). See the appendix in D. Hiro, *Black British White British* (Penguin, 1973); and R. Jenkins, *The Production of Knowledge at the Institute of Race Relations* (New Leader Press, 1971).

45 See the valuable collection of readings in C. R. Hensman, *From Gandhi to Guevara* (Allen Lane, 1970).

46 George Jackson, *Soledad Brother* (Penguin, 1971), pp. 217, 250.

47 Malcolm X, *By Any Means Necessary* (see 1 above), pp. 154–5.

JEREMY HARRISON

The Homeless and the Houseless

Summer 1971. A hostel for homeless families in the London borough of Southwark : Chaucer House. The poet would not be flattered. It is a huge, crumbling tenement block. Ray ran the tenants' association and lived in a two-room-and-kitchen flat with his wife and three children :

'They say it's a temporary address, but in this business if you're homeless you're helpless. We got evicted. Overcrowded. The cheapest place we got offered that would take kids was £14 a week. There were two kids then. It's a handicap in life, kids.

'I said to the welfare, "Why does a family have to be evicted before they can be helped by the welfare?" '

Ray's wife said : 'All they offer is to take your kids off you.'

Mary-Ann was in another flat. An unsupported mother of two little girls aged seven and two.

'I've been here five weeks. I had four rooms in Dulwich and a small . . . well, like a scullery. It was £6 a week rent and I had £12 from the Social Security. I was O.K. with the rent. But then you leave it a week and where are you? They say that this is a roof over your head and you have to take things, but this'll be my last week in here. I feel as if I'm a criminal and I've been put here to serve a sentence.

'My baby Carol, for two weeks she hasn't stopped going to the toilet and Linda, she had fleas for the first two weeks we were here. It's not so much that. It's the way you feel yourself. Slowing-down pills, I keep taking them. What've I done to end up in a place like this? I have to go to a friend's place for a bath.'

Spring 1972. A caravan site at Bordon in Hampshire. Many of the families in the eighty or so vans have gone to live there of their own accord, but fifteen or twenty of them have gone there because they were homeless, though they have never been officially admitted to be in need of temporary accommodation. Hampshire County Council officials have just advised them to go there, and in many cases have arranged accommodation for them and then driven them there from different corners of the county. It is one of those cases where one can be pretty certain that the only thing which prevents them being officially defined as homeless is the fact that Hampshire has insufficient temporary accommodation for them. If they lived in one of the Inner London Boroughs they would probably end up in bed and breakfast accommodation. In Hampshire it's likely to be a caravan site. One or two of the families had been there as long as nine years. Several for four or six years. And that on a slum site in caravans only designed to be lived in during the warm summer months.

My notes on three of the families read :

'It is nine years since Jim and Anne and their four children came to the site. The welfare officials who took them there said it was the only place available. Their caravan is small and the conditions are cramped. Bob who is almost fifteen, and Sally who is ten, have to share a bed. Susan aged six, and Betty aged five, sleep on cushions on the floor.

'The site was a last resort for Bill and Mary and their four young children. Until he left the army they had lived in quarters, but then they had to leave them. They looked for a home in Essex but couldn't find anything. Finally they came to the site. The welfare paid the deposit on their van. Bill now earns £19.20 a week basic, plus overtime. The rent for the van is £5.20 a week and £2 for electricity. The van leaks, and the kitchen is badly in need of re-decorating. One of the window panes falls out, and when they told the landlord he told them to stick it up with black tape. There is no heating in the van, which is a summer van. The landlord refused to provide heating so they had to buy their own heaters. The van isn't even sited properly. It is still on jacks.

'Alice, who is separated from her husband, came to the site six years ago. She says that the welfare brought her and her three children from Havant. She comes from Scotland, and could perhaps get herself a council house in Edinburgh. She was offered a house in Southampton but has decided she now belongs to the area and is waiting for her turn on the local list. She pays £5.30 a week for her van. Two of her four children are at a special school for asthmatics. When they are home for their holidays they have to share a bedroom six feet square with the younger children.'

All these people have been completely homeless. They are among a constantly growing number of families who suffer each year from the housing shortage, especially in London, and from the insecurity of privately rented accommodation. Nearly all of them have become homeless because they have been evicted by private landlords, in many cases simply because they had children. On any night of the year there are more than 20,000 people in hostels for the homeless in England and Wales. There are more than 6,000 children in the care of local authorities, separated from their parents for no other reason than that there is no family home to which they can go.

There are two faces of homelessness: the literally houseless, who never come to the notice of the authorities and are therefore far worse off than those who are actually living in hostels; and the homeless, if you take the word 'home' to imply more than just a roof and four walls.

Most of us now accept that the quality of the roof and the stability of the walls is pretty crucial too, as is the state of the drainage, the condition of the wiring and the quality of the immediate environment. Some, and I count myself one of them, maintain that a slum is no home. Life in a slum is so warped and constrained by slum conditions and the stresses these place on the family that it can't be called properly civilized. It is not conducive to health, or education or happiness. It imposes tremendous physical burdens and mental burdens which grow rather than diminish as the majority of us find our lives becoming more comfortable, as the gap between the rich and the poor widens.

At the centre of many large cities—London, Glasgow, Liverpool, Manchester, Newcastle, Edinburgh, Birmingham, Cardiff, Bradford, the list is a long one—there are enclaves of condemned or degenerating slum property.

The Government's sample Housing Stock Survey, carried out during 1971 and published in 1972, suggests that out of a total stock of just over 17,000,000 homes no fewer than 1,200,000 are unfit for human habitation. Altogether, no less than 2,900,000 lack one or more of the basic amenities of a fixed bath, sole use of an inside W.C. and hot water at three points.

It does seem that clearance and improvement are at last beginning to make some sort of impact on these figures, and the Government has said that 700,000 of the unfit houses are inside present clearance areas, which means that there are firm plans to dispose of them. But the other 500,000 are likely to prove infinitely more difficult to clear, and one must remember that fresh properties are deteriorating each year. Estimates of the number of such deteriorating houses vary, but no one seriously suggests fewer than 75,000 a year, and nobody has challenged Shelter's 1971 estimate of 200,000 a year. This was based on the age of the total housing stock and the likely rate of obsolescence.

The Government's estimates of improvement also disregard two other known dangers. The first is that a number of council estates built since the war (no one knows how many as yet) are already becoming slums. This is not so much because the housing was built to unsatisfactory specifications, but because it was ineptly planned and insensitively administered. The communities have degenerated because of the bad planning, and the housing is rapidly degenerating in the face of inadequate maintenance, too many changes of tenants, and unreasonable wear. Some, like a number of high-rise blocks, will become slums because of structural design defects.

The second danger is that a substantial number of the houses which have been converted and improved with the aid of Improvement Grants will not last the course they were planned for because the work was substandard. There are fears that a considerable number of the conversions done by housing associations in 1969 and 1970 will be slums within ten or fifteen years. Standards have risen a good deal since those early days. In some cases they needed to. These figures mean that at a conservative estimate there are a million families in conditions officially described as 'unfit'. They mean that it is most unlikely that the Government's prediction that the slums will be cleared by 1980 can be fulfilled, and anyone who assumes such a thing is dangerously wrong.

If the extent of the problem is horrifying enough, its deeper implications are catastrophic. We shall still be dealing with ruined lives and the results of smothered opportunity a generation and more after we have finished providing decent housing.

Of course slum housing goes to the poor. Of course they are homeless. Naturally enough, where the housing in a community is seriously decayed, the roads, the drains and the other physical services will be equally bad. If there is unemployment, the slums and the hostels for the homeless will contain more than their share of the victims. Health will be poor. Schools will be badly equipped, and the lack of academic achievement will reflect the poverty of the families and the lack of study facilities in the houses. Energy is sapped by the arduous mechanics of maintaining basic living standards, leaving none over for improvement, none for escape.

Slum communities are regions of multiple deprivation. Their life can be improved by fresh housing; it must be improved by fresh housing, for nothing of value can be done without it. But nothing complete and permanent can be done without a concerted programme of improvement in every facet of life, work and welfare. Poverty and deprivation in the inner city is a complex network of needs which dictates a comprehensive network of matching solutions.

But the families themselves tell the story best. Their predicament has changed very little in more than two years, except that if anything they have become relatively poorer, less able to ameliorate their conditions and compensate for their hardships.

Autumn 1970 : Vincent Crescent, Birmingham. It has since been demolished. When we went there it was scheduled for demolition in late 1972 or early 1973, and until then it was being used by the Corporation to house poor families. As a result of pressure (though Birmingham Corporation never admitted this to be the case) Vincent Crescent was demolished by the end of 1971. Of the two families I refer to here one was rehoused through Shelter's housing association contacts, and the other, eventually, by Birmingham Corporation.

Vincent Crescent was a gloomy little curve of houses. It was probably built by one of the big Birmingham breweries around 1860. By

1970 the houses were in an appalling condition and since demolition had been 'imminent' for years, nothing had been done about them. Roofs were slipping and falling into holes, gutters hanging, floors collapsing, walls falling in. Each of the houses had two rooms downstairs, two upstairs and an unusable attic. There were no inside lavatories, no baths, no hot water. Most of the outside lavatories were in a state of collapse.

Joy, 35, and her husband Tony, 32, had three children aged four, three and eighteen months. He had been going progressively blind and from holding down a job as a spot welder at between £30 and £40 a week he had drifted into unemployment with a total income of £10.15 a week. From a decent council house they had sunk to the bottom of the ladder, leaving a pile of rent arrears at every stage. Before Birmingham Corporation would allow the housing association to rehouse them Shelter had to pay almost £200 in accumulated rent arrears. Ransom money. Joy said: 'Christmas is just like any other day of the week. You don't play on it too much with the kids, like about Father Christmas. You don't mention that. You don't ask them what they want. She said the other day that she wants a push chair and a doll. Some hopes. I'll tell you. We'll be freezed out of here if it snows. There's terrible draughts. It's the kids you worry about. They've been bad since we came here. They've got terrible chests. There's rats in the house next door. The kids came in and said, "There's a funny cat with a great long tail", and we went outside and it was a bloody big rat. The kitchen gets soaked, and that wall. But it's not that bad. I say I'm not that badly off. And the cellar gets flooded and the sink blocks up. I think that's what makes the kids bad. It doesn't matter what germ you get, everybody in the street gets it every time. There's so much dirt. That's where you miss a bathroom, with the kids. We get the black beetles in here. He has to burn them. I'm out on the street as soon as they come. They're from the cellar.'

Joy said that she thought it was worst for the children and in the long run she was probably right. But in the main the children accepted the conditions better than their parents. The plight of the children was, and still is, the real horror, but the parents felt it most keenly on behalf of their children.

Further down Vincent Crescent lived Sally, who was then eleven years old. She lived with her mother and two of her brothers in a house identical to Joy and Tony's. The house was the same, but the conditions were worse. More water came in, the front door was so ill-fitting and so rotten that it provided little protection. Sally was an exception among the children in that she was bitterly aware of both the poverty and the squalor. I started off by asking her about Christmas: 'Half the kids up this street don't have that many toys. Like last Christmas, that was horrible. We didn't even have that many clothes. I was too frightened to eat my dinner with the cockroaches. For presents I had a book and crayons and a box of sweets from the school. I wish I was out of here. My friends at school, they all live in maisonettes. Everybody in my class lives in a maisonette except me and another girl. You've got to have new furniture to move into one of them. The worst thing about living here is the cockroaches and the rats. I've seen them, yes. Running under the table here. I found a mouse in the bowl we wash in and I killed it with a broom.'

Summer 1971 : Salford. Hard by Coronation Street itself, a block of housing lying between the Lower Broughton Road and the River Irwell. Most of the housing was of the two-up two-down variety. Some had a bathroom and hot water, but they were a minority. Lavatories were in the back yards. The condition of the housing and the condition of the tenants fell into three distinct categories, always visible in these areas of decaying urban property, but unusually well defined in Salford. A number of the houses were in extremely good condition, with painted steps, respectable brickwork and neat curtains on show. These belonged to the old people and the families who had lived there all their lives. Horrified by what was happening to the area, they cut themselves off and struggled to preserve their standards and their dignity amid the encroaching decay. The majority of the houses were in a state of medium decay : in disrepair, poorly furnished, badly curtained. In the main they contained young families who were there for no other reason than that they could not afford any of the more acceptable council accommodation. They had more children than the average, less money than the average. Their houses were in a bad condition because they had not been properly maintained and they had suffered the wear and tear of too many sets of tenants, none of whom intended staying longer than they had to. The council would not repair them and the tenants could not afford to. A few houses were little better than crumbling ruins, tenanted by what councils call 'problem families'. Perhaps that is not the right phrase, but by the time families get to that stage, no simple label can be adequate. The fact is that they can no longer be helped by conventional means. They are completely withdrawn from the world. Intoxicated and befuddled by their own hopelessness, they live in the most appalling filth and misery. They wreck houses and break social workers' hearts. Nobody has yet found a way to help them.

Jane had been in her house for eighteen months. She and her husband had three children. Jane was in her middle twenties, but if you met her in a nice middle-class suburb you'd take her for thirty-five at least. How many women are lonely? It is a problem not confined to the slums, but it must be worse when there are no mitigating comforts. Jane was lonely, and anxious to talk : 'We've got the back kitchen, and that's not much. Then there's this room, the front room and two bedrooms. They're not damp, but I'm afraid to shut the children's bedroom door because all the bricks are coming down. They're terrible these places because they should have been pulled down years ago. Before this we were in a flat, and it was a two-roomed flat, and then they got us this place, but it wasn't worth it. It's the first corporation place we've had and we've been on the council list for four years. There's no bath, no hot water. As far as I can make out from the neighbours they're up for another seven years.' Her eldest child was three and her youngest six months. Had they been able to improve the house at all? 'Everything you put up just comes down,' she said. 'The floor's all rotten. Every time you put lino down it just spoils. We've got lots of mice and beetles. There's no windows in the kitchen so when I cook the steam brings all the paper down. We've got a plastic bath and I have to boil kettles of water for it.'

They were in furnished rooms for about three years, she said, where they paid £4.50 a week rent. Their new rent was much less than that but they hadn't paid it for some time. They were hoping the council would evict them and find them somewhere else. An odd line of reasoning, but based on the assumption that the council would find it difficult to find them anywhere as bad. This sort of mistaken rent protest is a common thing, and it adds incredible complications to a family's relationship with its local council. It usually ends with a capitulation on the part of the family, which is then faced with the daunting prospect of paying off a substantial sum in arrears. Many families whom councils refuse to move from slums into reasonable housing because of their rent arrears begin to withhold money in this sort of protest.

Jane went on : My husband's not working. He wants to get himself a night job. He gets work at a warehouse more than anything, but what he picks up there he can get more on the dole.' In fact her husband's situation was more complex than that. He had left her, then he had returned. But she was still drawing money from Social Security on the basis of his desertion. 'But I'm not drawing any money I shouldn't be,' she said. She thought it all evened out in the end.

'If they evict us,' she said hopefully, 'they'll put me and the children in the Homestead. That's like an old people's home, but they put mothers and children there. It's all substandard stuff they put you in once they evict you. But whatever it is it's got to be better than this.' She had just begun a part-time job. She was trying it out. It involved putting the thread into Christmas gift tags. She had brought three boxes home to begin with, and the deal was that if she threaded every tag in those boxes she would get £5. That worked out at £1 for every 3,000 tags.

On the other side of the road, in exactly the same size house, lived Anne and her family. They were far more cramped. There were her husband, a boy of fourteen, a boy of eleven, a boy of ten, a girl of nine, a boy of six, and a girl of three. They had been there for eight years. This means that they arrived before the council bought the houses from their private owners. 'According to what they say, we've still got seven years left in these places,' she said. 'They are just not fit to live in. They're moving all the riff-raff in. It was a private landlord when we came in. Then the bay window rained in and the back kitchen wall was no good. I've never been able to use the little back bedroom because it just pours down the wall. We've spent all we can on it. We can't do any more and that's it. According to the council I need four bedrooms and there aren't any houses with that many. So we've got to wait until they get one.'

In the meantime she put all the children but the youngest into the one dry bedroom, and she and her husband and the three year old slept on a folding settee in the living-room. They had been on the housing list since they married fourteen years before but never came to the top because they did not realize that they should re-register each year.

'A man came here four or five years ago and said he was from the housing and could he look at the house. I said "What are you here for?", and he said, "You're on the transfer list." I thought that meant we'd get a house, but we haven't heard anything. There's no hot water here. There's nothing for the kids. I have to fill the tub up. When I do that it takes two hours. It takes you half an hour to boil each lot of water. I have to put two of them in and then empty it and then put another two in. When the big lad wants a bath we have to wait until the others have gone to bed, and then my husband has to go out. When I have a bath they all have to go out. There's no privacy in these houses.

'The first two years the baby was never away from the doctor's. It's just the sleeping conditions. We pay the council £1.38 a week rent. There's nothing here really. There's only an outside toilet, and they're no good round here. Half of them leak.'

She came back to the bathing problems, which were made much worse by the fact that her husband was a coalman, and therefore needed a bath every night. He had to wait until last, sometimes until eleven or twelve o'clock. But it meant that they could never have visitors because he was never clean in time to receive them.

'I manage. I just manage. And neither of us go out, ever. We've had just one holiday since we were married. You can't save on £15 a week. He gets £21 before stoppages, and then he has £2 and I have £15. We're not eligible for Supplementary Benefit. I don't get no free milk, but I get free dinners for four of them, but the eldest won't stay at school for his dinner. But we manage all right as far as meals are concerned. It's just the sleeping and the hot water that you miss. According to the corporation there's much worse than this in Salford, God help them. Mind you, you see on the telly where they've got rats. I think I'm bloody lucky. I haven't got anything like that.'

Summer 1972: Splott, Cardiff. Splott is a jigsaw-piece-shaped district of Victorian housing close to the centre of Cardiff. On the east it is bounded by marshes and land reclaimed from the Bristol Channel, on the south-west by a steelworks, and on the north by the main Cardiff to Newport railway line. In the south and west of the ward the property is in bad condition. In the north-east it is much sounder. Cardiff Corporation has begun its slow demolition process, clearing street by street from the south. The very worst conditions keep a few streets north of the bulldozer the whole time.

Joan and Bill went to their house thirteen years ago. Then they had a six-month-old baby, and they had been walking the streets.

BILL: 'When it rains it all comes in. The water all comes through on the landing. All the bedrooms are leaking and the chairs have gone rotten.'

JOAN: 'The wall outside the children's bedroom window all fell down into the street. It was blown down by the wind. We heard a bang and it had fallen out onto the pavement. It could have killed someone.'

Three of the bedrooms and one of the downstairs rooms were completely unusable because of damp.

JOAN: 'The children get filthy round here and it's a problem having no bath. I've got to get a bungalow bath in the kitchen to bath them and then I boil up the water in buckets.'

BILL: 'The dirt here's terrible. I've got trouble with my throat and glands, and I mustn't work where there's dust, but you breathe it all out in the street.'

He had been unemployed for five years. They were receiving £17.50 a week and paying almost £2 a week rent. One of their main worries was the eldest boy's education.

JOAN: 'He's staying on at school until he's seventeen. He has to do his homework in the front room. He's very keen on biology.'

Summer 1972: Bradford: A row of large old houses in the Manningham ward, the worst part of the city where many of the houses are in an advanced state of decay. Some have been purchased by Asian immigrants. The houses are much larger than the average, so have tended to be split up into single furnished rooms. Their condition varies, but in the main they are damp and crumbling.

Jack and Kay had a room in one of them for themselves and their two boys aged five and eleven. They'd been there for nearly a year.

KAY : 'We moved because the other conditions were a damned sight worse. There were no cooking facilities, no bath and no toilets. There's a bath in here. Everybody shares. There's ten other than us in the house. There's a bathroom with a toilet and a separate toilet. We pay £3.25 a week. Ours are the only children in the house. We're not going to stay here. Not if we can get somewhere else. But it's difficult. You can't save money because he's sick and waiting to go back into hospital. We'd like a house, anything. With two bedrooms and a cellar kitchen. I don't want owt fantastic, but you can't get houses to rent. We're not on the council list because quite honestly we can't afford the rents. We've no privacy whatever. You go into the bathroom even to change and there's someone at the door waiting to come in.'

JACK : 'I think there's work round here for anyone who wants it. But I've been out sick for nearly two and a half years. And if you tell me you can save out of sick brass I'd like to know how. The place we came from was really disgusting. There was no windows and we paid £4.50. It was near the park and if you wanted to go to the toilet you had to go to the park. It's certainly a problem them both being in the same room with us here. And there again he's eleven you know and I don't think it's right him being in the same room.'

KAY : 'I go to work seven mornings and two evenings a week, but it just about pays the rent. We live on what Jack gets.'

JACK : 'That's about £19 a week in all. In work it would be £30.'

KAY : 'I think one of the things that's suffered is that the oldest boy is of above average intelligence but he's nowhere to study. He's in the first ninety of Bradford schools for the scholarship, but he's no privacy.'

Summer 1972 : Edinburgh, Central Leith. In the tradition of Scottish tenement development. The effect is by no means as universally horrifying as in Glasgow, but many of the individual properties are no better. The situation of many of the families is as bad.

Sandra and Michael had been in their two-room apartment for fourteen years. They have two sons aged five and six, and two daughters of nine and fifteen. Sandra said : 'I need a four-room apartment with the two boys and two girls. The Corporation must have owned this place for about eight years, I think. Our first interview for a new house was two years ago. The wall by the door —I've never papered that, it's all soaking. It's not worth doing anything to it when we're waiting for a house. They're breaking the windows round here every night. If they think a house is empty they'll break the windows.'

Their elder daughter had just left school and they were pessimistic about finding her a job. Michael himself had been out of work for more than two years, and had only just managed to get work as a cleaner at a bus station. Most of the families had already been moved out of their tenement. They were anxious to go but frightened of some of the possibilities. 'I don't want underfloor heating if possible,' said Sandra, 'because you get all those big bills and get into difficulty.' In the meantime : 'The street lights are not on. And I'm going to try and get them to put some lights on the stairs.'

These were the lives, the problems, the hopes of eleven families, collected in a space of two years. Some who were homeless have been housed. Some who lived in slums have moved on to better things. In some cases they've moved because their turn has come around. In other cases Shelter made enough fuss to ensure that they received priority.

But homelessness increases. The slums decrease, but far too slowly, and the process of fresh decay is constant : more properties, more areas. More poor families find themselves 'selected' by their poverty to live in slums. More families who have been in slums all their lives realize that yet another generation has been wasted in the blight that touches almost every facet of life.

We could, of course, clear the slums. We could dispose of the problem of homelessness. Both would cost a great deal of money, but it could be found. What is lacking is neither the cash nor the expertise. It is the will to do so. The slums are isolated within the cities that harbour them. People have not been forced to know about them. They have not had to care. Most people still do not care.

FRANK FIELD

The New Poor : A Statistical Analysis

1 A Historical Perspective

The first social investigator in this country to define the term
'poverty' with any precision was Seebohm Rowntree. He used a twofold definition :

> Families living in poverty may be divided into two sections; one,
> families whose total earnings are insufficient to obtain the maxi-
> mum necessaries for the maintenance of mere physical efficiency.
> Poverty falling under this head may be described as 'primary
> poverty'. Two, families whose total earnings would be sufficient
> for the maintenance of mere physical efficiency were it not that
> some proportion of it is absorbed by other expenditure, either
> useful or wasteful. Poverty falling under this head may be de-
> scribed as 'secondary poverty'.[1]

This distinction between poverty caused by inadequate income
on the one hand, and personal failings on the other, has dogged our
discussions ever since. Throughout this chapter, poverty is defined
as a lack of financial resources. Discussion about secondary poverty
has been left to after-dinner speech makers.

The following diagram plots the findings of Rowntree's first
study of the extent of poverty in York. It can be seen that the
largest group living below the poverty-line were families where the
head of the household was in work but earning a poverty wage.
That finding is as true today as it was when Rowntree's report was
published in the first days of the twentieth century.

IMMEDIATE CAUSES OF POVERTY

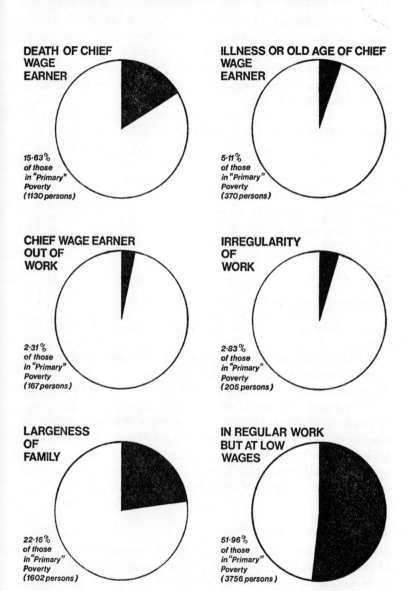

**DEATH OF CHIEF
WAGE
EARNER**

15·63%
of those
in "Primary"
Poverty
(1130 persons)

**ILLNESS OR OLD AGE OF CHIEF
WAGE
EARNER**

5·11%
of those
in "Primary"
Poverty
(370 persons)

**CHIEF WAGE EARNER
OUT OF
WORK**

2·31%
of those
in "Primary"
Poverty
(167 persons)

**IRREGULARITY
OF
WORK**

2·83%
of those
in "Primary"
Poverty
(205 persons)

**LARGENESS
OF
FAMILY**

22·16%
of those
in "Primary"
Poverty
(1602 persons)

**IN REGULAR WORK
BUT AT LOW
WAGES**

51·96%
of those
in "Primary"
Poverty
(3756 persons)

Source: B.S.Rowntree , Poverty: A Study of Town Life (Macmillan 1901), page 121.

INTER-WAR STUDIES

Rowntree's definition of poverty was used in all the inter-war studies, although for his survey in 1936 he added to the list of necessities, 'thereby making the definition slightly more generous as a concession to the increasing prosperity'. Table 1 summarizes the results of studies which were carried out by members of university social science departments.

Table 1: INCIDENCE OF POVERTY BEFORE THE WAR

	Working-class households	
Survey	Families in poverty %	Children in poverty %
London 1929	9.8	13.0
Merseyside 1929–31	17.3	24.5
Southampton 1931	21.3	30.0
Sheffield 1933	15.4	26.9
Miles Platting 1933	9.0	28.0
Plymouth 1935	16.5	–
York 1936	31.1	43.0
Bristol 1937	10.7	21.4
Birmingham (Kingstanding) 1939	14.0	31.0

SOURCE: *Poverty: 10 Years After Beveridge* (PEP, 1952).

In the studies conducted during the late twenties and early thirties unemployment, inadequate wages, old age, widowhood and sickness were the major causes of poverty. The surveys conducted at the end of the decade, when the employment position had begun to improve, found that large families were the major cause of poverty. For working-class parents to have three or more children before the war was practically enough to guarantee poverty.[2] It was against this background that Beveridge wrote his inter-departmental report on 'Social Insurance and Allied Services' in 1942.

THE POST-WAR YEARS

Beveridge's aim was to abolish want. To do this he set out a number of policies aimed at guaranteeing (a) the people in work and (b) those unable to work, an income above the poverty-line. Even though he defined the subsistence level in a stricter manner than

Rowntree in 1936, the Labour Government did not fully implement his proposals. However, it is important to look briefly at Beveridge's scheme.

First, there were the proposals to abolish poverty caused by low earnings. These were based on the assumption that every male wage-earner earned enough to support himself, a wife and one child, as well as being able to cover an average rent payment. We have since learned that this assumption, if true in 1942, is no longer so today.[5] Beveridge therefore proposed that family allowances, a benefit which would cover the cost of raising a child, should begin with the second child. In calculating the size of this payment, which was originally set at 40p a week, Beveridge assumed that school dinners would be free to all children.

Secondly, the Social Insurance and Allied Services Report advocated a system of national insurance benefits to which every member of the community would become eligible. However, eligibility would only be granted after claimants had fulfilled the qualifying conditions, so the scheme envisaged a transitional period when many of the poor would be dependent on some form of means-tested public assistance. As contribution records were established, fewer and fewer would come into this category, and Beveridge envisaged that the National Assistance Board (which replaced the Unemployment Assistance Board) would slowly wither away and become an unimportant part of our social security system.

Again, the second stage of the Beveridge proposals were not fully implemented. Insurance benefits were not set at a level above the poverty-line. As most people have few or no resources to fall back on when they are unable to work, a growing army of claimants became, and remained, dependent on drawing a means-tested subsistence allowance. In 1966, the National Assistance Board was replaced by the Supplementary Benefits Commission. Today, nearly 5 million claimants have their income and livelihood dependent wholly or partly on supplementary benefits payments. Table 2 sets out the number of claimants drawing a means-test allowance in 1948, and the equivalent data for 1971. From this it can be seen that there has been very nearly a 300 per cent increase in the numbers dependent on a means-tested supplement. By no stretch of the imagination can this be described as a withering-away of the National Assistance Board.

Table 2: NUMBERS DEPENDENT ON NATIONAL ASSIST-
ANCE IN 1948 AND UPON SUPPLEMENTARY
BENEFIT IN 1971

	No. of regular allowances (thousands)		Total number of persons provided for in
	1948	1971	1971
All Supplementary Benefits	1,011	2,909	4,564
All Supplementary Pensions	638	1,919	2,310
retirement pensions and N.I. widows over 60	495	1,816	2,200
others over pensionable age	143	103	110
All Supplementary Allowances	–	990	2,254
unemployed with N.I. benefits	19	129	384
„ without N.I. „	34	258	608
sick and disabled with N.I. benefits	80	146	297
sick and disabled without N.I. benefits	64	159	183
N.I. widows under 60	81	65	104
Women with dependent children	32	213	635
Others	63	20	41

SOURCE: For 1948 figures, see *Social Trends*, vol. I (HMSO, 1970), p. 48.
For 1971 figures, see DHSS Annual Report (HMSO, 1972).

POVERTY TODAY

Each autumn Parliament approves the level of income for claimants
dependent on supplementary benefit. Many regard this as the
official definition of poverty. It certainly provides us with a generally
accepted yardstick for discussion on the numbers in poverty. The
latest supplementary benefit scale rates are to be found in Table 3.

Table 3: SUPPLEMENTARY BENEFIT RATES IN 1972–3
(WEEKLY)

	£
Married couple	10.65
Single person	6.55
Under 5	1.90
5–10	2.25
11–12	2.75
13–15	3.40
16–17	4.05
18–20	5.20

On top of their personal allowance, each household dependent on supplementary benefit usually receives a sum to cover the rent in full. So a married man with two children, one under five and the other ten, paying a rent of £3, will receive a supplementary benefit allowance of £17.80 a week. This, then, is the poverty-line for a family of that size paying that rent with children of that age.

2 Living Below the Poverty-Line

Although the Supplementary Benefits Commission provides a minimum income, seven groups live on resources which are less than the officially-defined poverty-line and in this section I look at each in turn.

POVERTY WAGES

The largest group living below the poverty-line is that of wage-earners and their families who earn their poverty, i.e. where the family income from work is less than that family's supplementary benefit entitlement. In 1971, the Government published the 'Report on Two Parent Families', which gave a detailed analysis of the low-income groups of the 1968, 1969 and 1970 Family Expenditure Surveys. It looked at the number of families with incomes less than their supplementary benefit entitlement, together with families whose combined resources just lifted them above the statutory poverty-line. The following table (4) gives details on the number of these families. At the end of 1970, one per cent of working families lived at an income below the supplementary benefit level, while over 11 per cent were within £5 of it. Further details on the working poor can be found in Table 4 and in Section 3 (pp. 54-6).

THOSE ELIGIBLE FOR BUT NOT CLAIMING SUPPLEMENTARY BENEFIT

Interpreting the survey results published in *The Aged in the Welfare State* (1962), Townsend and Wedderburn estimated that 11 per cent of old people were eligible for supplementary benefit but had not applied. Soon afterwards two Government reports confirmed the

Table 4: WORKING FAMILIES ON OR BELOW THE
POVERTY-LINE

	Number of children in family				All families
Less than £5 above SB	1	2	3	4 or more	
Number of families (thousands)	237	229	134	135	735
Proportion of families	9.8%	10.1%	13.6%	19.6%	11.3%
Less than £2 above SB Number of families (thousands)	53	50	46	55	204
Proportion of families	2.2%	2.2%	4.6%	5.6%	2.9%
Below SB level Number of families (thousands)	28	3	20	23	74
Proportion of families	1.2%	0.1%	2.0%	2.2%	1.0%

SOURCE (and for further information): see David Piachaud's 'A Profile of Family Poverty' in *Poverty*, 19 (CPAG, 1971).

dimensions of the problem. In 1965 the Allen Committee of Inquiry into the 'Impact of Rates on Households' found 'about half a million retired households . . . apparently eligible for assistance but not getting it'. This estimate was revised upwards in the 'Financial and Other Circumstances of Retirement Pensioners' report. The report estimated 700,000 households as eligible for National Assistance but not claiming it. These households contained about 850,000 people, or about 14 per cent of all retirement pensioners.

Concern over these findings led to the replacement of the National Assistance Board by the Supplementary Benefits Commission. The change in name was accompanied by a massive advertising drive aimed at persuading the poor of their right to benefit. As a result, the numbers claiming SB increased. And so was founded the belief that the introduction of supplementary benefits in 1966 cut dramatically the numbers of poor eligible for benefit but not receiving it. However, such optimism not supported by Tony Atkinson in his book *Poverty in Britain and the Reform of Social Security*.[4] He examined the introduction of the 1966 Social Security Act and concluded that many of those eligible for benefit were not claiming it, even though a massive advertising campaign on the right to benefit was launched soon after the Bill received Royal Assent. 'On an optimistic view, the reduction in number not claiming the assistance to which they were entitled was only a quarter of those found to be not claiming by the Ministry's inquiry in 1965.' The author adds that it is possible that because of the higher assistance scales, the proportion of those eligible who claim may actually have fallen since 1966. So, despite legislation and publicity, there are still 600,000 old people, quite apart from additional numbers becoming eligible for supplementary assistance for the first time since the 1966 Act, who are eligible for assistance under this means-tested programme but not claiming it. These represented about 27 per cent of persons eligible for assistance.

The Circumstances of Families report of 1966 found others entitled to supplementary benefit who were not obtaining it, either through pride or ignorance of their rights. Of families with two or more children where the father was sick or unemployed, a third were getting supplementary benefit but 35,000, or one in four, though apparently entitled, were not obtaining it. Failure to claim was particularly common where the father had been sick for less than three months; two-thirds of those entitled to supplementary benefits were not drawing it. Further, about 10,000 fatherless families were entitled to supplementary benefit but were not receiving it. Most of them had incomes of at least £2 a week below the minimum.[5] The numbers given for unemployed and sick fathers, as well as fatherless families were based on the National Assistance scale in force in mid-1966. Many more families would have qualified when the higher supplementary benefit scale was introduced in the latter part of that year.

WAGE STOPPED

In the Supplementary Benefits Commission's report, 'Administration of the Wage Stop', the Minister of Social Security admitted that there was much misunderstanding of what the wage stop is. To quote the report : 'The wage stop does not require a man to get less when receiving supplementary benefit than he would get when working. What it does is to ensure that an unemployed man's income is no *greater* than it would be if he were in full-time employment.' So the poor in work are kept at below subsistence level when they cease work and are forced to draw supplementary benefit. It is

not surprising, therefore, that in their report on the life style of
fifty-two families, the Commission found that 'the general impression derived from visits was not so much one of grinding poverty
in any absolute sense as one of unrelieved dreariness with, in some
cases, little hope of improvement in the future.'[6]

In most of the families visited, the father was over thirty and
there were three or more children. Most of the fathers had been out
of work for more than a year. Indeed some had been out of work
for five years or more. The majority had done labouring work in
the past and the potential net earnings of most of them were estimated at around £9.50 to £11.50 a week. The larger the number
of children, the greater a man's supplementary benefit entitlement,
so the wage stop operated most viciously against the poor with
large families. The amount of the wage stop deduction ranged from
under 50p to over £6. In the majority of cases the deduction was
£2.50 or less.

As one would expect, diet varied a great deal among the fifty-two
families. Several mothers said they had difficulty in finding money
for food on the two days preceding payment of their allowances. In
most cases fresh meat was only bought at weekends, and items such
as fruit, biscuits and cakes were often mentioned as something
families had to do without. Most of the families commented on the
lack of variety in their diet and said that bread and potatoes were
eaten in large quantities.

Clothing was found to be generally poor, and most mothers said
that keeping the children in shoes caused considerable difficulty.
Similarly, stocks of bedclothes were low and in some cases they were
almost non-existent. A third of the families told the Commission
that they had had the gas or electricity cut off at some time in the
past and a quarter said they commonly ran short of fuel in the
winter. Possibly readers would consider this a little different from
'unrelieved dreariness'. Table 5 sets out the number of wage
stopped families since 1964.

COHABITATION

The Supplementary Benefits Commission believes that it has to
maintain equity between the female claimants drawing supplementary allowances and the wives of the low wage-earners. Is it fair for

Table 5: NUMBER OF NATIONAL ASSISTANCE SUP-
PLEMENTARY BENEFIT RECIPIENTS WITH A
WAGE STOP DEDUCTION EACH YEAR SINCE 1964

	Unemployed		Others	
Year	Number	Amount of weekly wage stop deduction	Number	Amount of weekly wage stop deduction
1964	13,960	1.30	2,600	1.27
1965	17,660	1.93	2,790	1.48
1967*	33,620	1.68	3,930	1.56
1968	29,530	1.42	2,880	1.61
1969	31,280	1.64	2,760	1.86
1970	33,190	1.95	2,430	2.39
1971	22,252	1.43	977	1.70

SOURCE: DHSS Annual Sample Inquiries.
* No inquiry held in 1966.

a female claimant to be living as a common-law wife, when the wife
of a low wage-earner is ineligible for supplementary benefit?

The SBC assures us that, in the vast majority of cases, no difficulties arise. Most couples entering a common-law marriage wish to
be regarded as husband and wife. But in some instances the SBC
have to decide whether a claimant is living as somebody else's wife.
According to the SBC's paper, Cohabitation, officers are supposed
to establish whether there is a common household, whether the
couple are known to be husband and wife in the neighbourhood,
what the sleeping arrangements are, whether the couple have children, whether the couple go on holiday together and so on. Readers
will be quick to realize how difficult it is to establish these facts
unless the special investigator is the cohabitee. (The first sixteen
special investigators or supplementary benefit policemen were appointed in 1954. By 1971 their numbers had swelled to 278.)

Welfare Rights organizations have come across a number of
cases where the allowances have been withdrawn unjustly. Unfortunately, we do not know in how many cases the Commission
acts wrongly. What we do know is the number of cases where, on
the grounds of cohabitation or fictitious desertion by the husband,
the Commission withdraws or reduces female claimants' allowances.
Details on this are set out in the table below.

C

Table 6: NUMBER OF BENEFICIARIES THOUGHT TO BE
COHABITING OR CLAIMING FICTITIOUS
DESERTION 1968–71

Year	Cases Investigated	Allowances withdrawn or reduced
1968	6,173	3,194
1969	7,497	3,551
1970	9,356	4,388
1971	10,521	4,712

SOURCE: Letters from the Supplementary Benefits Commission, May 1971
and September 1972.

WORK-SHY RULES

Under the 1948 National Assistance Act and the 1966 Ministry of
Social Security Act, the Commission have power to withdraw or reduce a claimant's allowance. This power has been thought necessary
in order to prevent claimants drawing allowances unnecessarily. Few
would deny the need for the Commission to have the powers necessary to prevent abuse. Taxpayers have a right to expect that their
money is being used properly. But the Commission also has the
responsibility to see that the claimant is not prevented from exercis-
ing his right to benefit. How, then, can these two opposing demands
be balanced?

Since 1951 the NAB and SBC's Annual Reports have catalogued
the growth in the control procedures against abuse. If a claimant is
thought to be work-shy, his allowance may be made conditional on
his attending a re-establishment centre where, in official jargon, he
will be 're-introduced' to a work routine. Another check has been
that allowances may be made conditional on the claimant under-
going a medical examination. Alternatively claimants may be sued
for non-maintenance of themselves and/or their family. Unemployment review officers, who interview claimants who have been unemployed for any length of time and then find work, were first
established in 1961. Then their numbers totalled ten. By the end of
1971, they had grown to 117.

In each of these control measures, the claimant's right is protected.
For example, before a claimant can be sent to a re-establishment
centre, the SBC has to present its case to an independent tribunal.

Only the tribunal has the power to make a claimant's allowance conditional on his attending a centre.

This delicate balance between the rights of the claimant and the prevention of fraud was destroyed in 1968. In June of that year, the minister responsible announced that where the Commission 'feel' that jobs are available, all single, fit, unskilled men under forty-five will have their allowance limited to four weeks. Then it will automatically be cut off. For married or skilled men with children, the period allowed is three months before the four-week rule is applied. Over the last two and a half years the rule has been applied to a quarter of a million claimants. Table 7 gives the relevant information since the introduction of the allowances in 1968.

Table 7: NUMBER OF CLAIMANTS GIVEN LIMITED ALLOWANCES OCTOBER 1968–JUNE 1972

Period	Initial Limitation of Allowance	Limitation of Allowance after three months	Appeals Total	Number Revised
14.10.68– 17.12.68	15,724	1,132	232	26
18.12.68– 23.12.69*	81,784	6,140	1,108	146
24.12.69– 15.12.70	78,560	4,845	678	79
16.12.71	65,250	2,187	750	142
20.6.72	5,834	507	105	16

* Includes one week additional to the period covered in the Annual Report for 1969.
SOURCE: Correspondence between Lord Collison and CPAG, December 1971.

RENT STOPPED

As we have seen, a claimant's income is made up of his personal allowances plus a sum to cover the rent. Ever since 1948, the Commission has refused to meet some rents of claimants living in private accommodation. This has been done on the grounds that either the rent is unreasonable for the accommodation, or that it is unreasonable for the claimant to be living in such accommodation. Prior to 1959, maximum rent allowances were restricted to an amount fixed locally. In 1959 the fixed rent no longer applied and a reasonable rent could be met in full, but as Table 8 shows, an increasing number of rents have been classified as unreasonable. In this instance, as in all the others in this section, a claimant's income is reduced to below the poverty-line.

Table 8: NUMBER OF WEEKLY ALLOWANCES WITH UNMET RENT FOR EACH YEAR SINCE 1964

Year	Number with unmet rent	Average amount unmet per week	Percentage of householders	Total householders
1964	20,240	0.80	1.29	1,567,400
1965	18,420	0.88	1.15	1,604,470
1967*	18,760	0.95	0.87	2,154,150
1969*	22,710	1.09	0.99	2,295,990
1970	31,750	1.20	1.36	2,329,590
1971	31,760	1.05	1.28	2,471,950

* No inquiry held in 1966; not available in 1968.
SOURCE: DHSS Annual Special Sample Inquiries.

INDUSTRIAL MISCONDUCT

A claimant for supplementary benefit who is (a) disqualified from unemployment benefit because of industrial misconduct, voluntarily leaving his last job or refusal to take a suitable job, and (b) required to register for employment, will have his supplementary benefit reduced by 40 per cent for the first six weeks. This will mean a reduction of £2.30 a week below the statutory poverty-line. The number of reductions since 1955 are to be found in Table 9, although a note of warning needs to be made before interpreting the last column. Until the implementation of the Social Security Act 1971, there was only a 75p reduction of benefit. Figures for 1971 onwards will show a dramatic jump in the average amount of deductions.

3 Causes of Poverty

The vast majority of people are dependent on work, or on drawing benefit for their income. A minority are in a more privileged position and have their standard of living determined exclusively or in part by the income earned from capital holdings. Because wealth is so unevenly distributed, the vast majority of people do not share

Table 9: NUMBER OF VOLUNTARY UNEMPLOYED
DEDUCTIONS AT A DATE IN NOVEMBER OF
EACH YEAR SINCE 1955

| | Supplementary Benefit Unemployed Recipients* | | |
| | | | |
Year	Total	No. of reduced Allowances	% with a deduction	Average amount (of deduction)
1955	45,000	2,320	4.3	0.48
1956	64,000	3,000	4.7	0.63
1957	96,000	3,640	3.8	0.71
1958	151,000	6,880	4.6	0.70
1959	155,000	6,200	4.0	1.01
1960	128,000	5,080	4.0	0.96
1961	131,000	7,160	5.5	0.90
1962	202,000	9,800	4.9	1.10
1963	185,000	7,080	3.8	0.87
1964	131,000	4,800	3.7	1.16
1965	112,000	4,730	4.2	1.31
1966†				
1967	228,000	13,500	5.9	0.62
1968	225,000	14,590	6.5	0.63
1969	228,000	13,380	5.9	0.63
1970	240,000	14,580	6.1	0.63
1971	380,000	18,680	4.9	1.36

* Unemployment beneficiaries who register and are paid at the Employment
Exchange whether or not they are entitled to unemployment benefit.
† No inquiry held in 1966.
SOURCE: DHSS Annual Special Sample Inquiries.

this privilege, and they become poor either because they work for a
poverty wage, or are prevented from working and draw welfare
benefits valued at less than the official poverty-line. This section
looks at the main groups who, having no private resources, make up
the growing number of poor people in Britain.

LOW PAY

Firstly, what is meant by the term 'low pay'? A number of writers
have employed a rough definition of low pay.[7] They have used the
supplementary benefits scale for a family with two *or* three children
as the cut-off point between low paid and other workers. Apart from
its imprecision, there are two serious drawbacks to this approach.

The first is that between 1967 and 1972 the supplementary benefit scale rates were a falling proportion of average earnings (as they have been at other times as well). Consequently, any supplementary benefit definition of low paid will give a smaller proportion of workers as being low paid without any real improvement taking place in their living standards relative to their working colleagues. Moreover, the supplementary benefit scale rate for a husband, wife and two children, including an average rent payment, is only 39 per cent of average male industrial earnings. Few could believe that low pay would be abolished if we were successful in lifting wages above this meagre income level.

A more radical approach is to define low pay as earnings below a certain percentage of the average. At the moment, the lowest 10 per cent of male workers earn 67 per cent of median earnings. A target would be to raise the rewards of the lowest paid to 80 per cent of the median. Anyone earning less would be considered low paid.

Secondly who are the low paid?[8] The 1970 New Earnings Survey groups workers into different income bands. One band ends at £17, another £20. 80 per cent of average male industrial earnings in 1970 was £21.10. The £20 income band has, therefore, been taken as the cut-off point for low pay. It is then possible to look at (a) the percentage of the low paid in each industry, and (b) the distribution of low-paid workers between industries. Table 10 gives this information. Section A rates industries according to the number of low paid as a percentage of the total work force. Section B lists industries according to the number of low paid as a percentage of the total number of low paid in the economy. Readers will notice the consistency in the top ten ratings in both Sections A and B of industries such as agriculture, public administration, distribution and so on.

The extent to which low pay is a problem of Wages Council industries has been highlighted by the work of Incomes Data Services Ltd. In their September 1970 report, they made a comparison between pay increases and price increases for the low paid. Just as their August report had concluded that 'there can be no doubt from our evidence that Wages Council industries, as a group, are by far the worst off and that of the 32 groups in the lowest quarter, 24 were Wages Council industries', so this report spotlighted the deteriorating purchasing power for workers in Wages Council

Table 10: FULL-TIME MALE MANUAL WORKERS EARNING LESS THAN £20 PER WEEK IN APRIL 1971 (AGED 21 AND OVER, PAY NOT AFFECTED BY ABSENCE)

A: Incidence of low pay in each industry			B: % of all low-paid (nationally) employed in each industry		
Industry	%£20	Rank	Industry	%	Rank
Agriculture	43.8	1	Public Administration	11.2	1
Miscellaneous Services	33.9	2	Construction	11.1	2
Public Administration	29.4	3	Distribution	10.9	3
Professional & Scientific Services	28.4	4	Miscellaneous Services	10.6	4
			Transport & Communication	7.6	5
Distribution	26.1	5	Professional & Scientific Services	6.7	6
Ins. & Banking Services	22.6	6			
Leather, Leather Goods, Fur	22.2	7	Agriculture	6.1	7
Clothing & Footwear	21.1	8	Mechanical Engineering	4.1	8
Textiles	15.0	9	Textiles	3.6	9
Construction	13.4	10	Mining & Quarrying	3.3	10
Timber, Furniture etc.	11.8	11	Food, Drink & Tobacco	3.2	11
Instrument Engineering	10.1	12	Other Metal Goods	2.5	12
Other Manufacturing	9.9	13	Electrical Engineering	2.5	12
Mining & Quarrying	9.6	14	Metal Manufacture	1.9	14
Food, Drink & Tobacco	9.3	15	Ins. & Banking Services	1.8	15
Other Metal Goods	9.1	16	Clothing and Footwear	1.6	16
Electrical Engineering	8.2	17	Vehicles	1.6	16
Transport & Communication	8.2	17	Timber, Furniture etc.	1.5	18
Mechanical Engineering	7.1	19	Chemicals	1.5	18
Chemicals	6.6	20	Paper, Printing, Publishing	1.5	18
Bricks, Pottery, Glass etc.	6.1	21	Other Manufacturing	1.4	21
Paper, Printing etc.	5.6	22	Gas, Electricity & Water	1.1	22
Ships	5.5	23	Bricks, Pottery, Glasses etc.	1.1	22
Gas, Electricity & Water	5.1	24	Ships	0.6	24
Metal Manufacture	4.9	25	Instrument Engineering	0.5	25
Vehicles	3.2	26	Leather, Leather Goods, Fur	0.3	26
Coal & Petrol Products	1.3	27	Coal and Petrol Products	0.2	27
All Industries & Services	12.9			100.0	

SOURCE : Unpublished paper 'Industrial Distribution of Low Pay' by Stephen Winyard.

industries. In the five years up to the report's publication, retail prices rose by 24.7 per cent. During this period, in 25 out of 53 Wages Council industries the lowest minimum rates of pay for men rose by less than 24.7 per cent. From September 1968 to September 1970 prices rose by 12.1 per cent. In 30 of the 53 Wages Council industries pay had risen more slowly. But this analysis does not take account of price increases during the period under study. During the period August 1968 to July 1970, the Index of Retail Prices rose in 20 out of the 23 months. 'Thus workers who received pay increases equalling the rise in the cost of living over the period, in fact had their standard of living reduced throughout that period.'

A similar analysis was conducted by the Industrial Relations Review and Report. Dividing the negotiating groups into Wages Council and non-Wages Council establishments, the Report concluded that the problem of low basic rates of pay continues in most instances to be largely the problem of the Wages Council. Nine of the bottom 10, and 21 of the bottom 25 lowest-paying industrial groups are Wages Council industries. Wages Council industries remain the poor relations both by nature of the size of pay increases and the length of time between each increase.

THE UNEMPLOYED

In the July 1970 count on unemployment, just over half a million people were looking for employment. By January 1972, the numbers had doubled. But who are the unemployed? In which industries did they work? And in what part of the country do they live?

Table 11 classifies the unemployed according to their past employment. The first two classifications are the most important. The

Table 11: NUMBERS OF UNEMPLOYED, CLASSIFIED BY PREVIOUS WORK EXPERIENCE (SEPTEMBER 1971)

| | Men | | Women | |
Occupation	Wholly Unemployed	Notified Vacancies	Wholly Unemployed	Notified Vacancies
Labourers	326,486	7,140	–	–
Administrative, Professional and Technical Workers	45,314	10,487	8,075	8,922
Engineering and Allied Trade Workers	58,332	11,776	3,088	1,802
Transport and Communications	33,696	5,768	2,294	1,051
Service, Sport and Recreation	18,393	5,170	13,269	13,401
Shop Assistants	10,059	2,650	10,669	4,102
Clerical Workers	58,721	4,224	28,434	11,007
Other Workers	77,535	18,777	38,613	18,410
TOTAL	628,536	65,992	104,442	58,695

SOURCE : British Labour Statistics (HMSO, 1971).

second, recording the numbers of unemployed administrative, professional and technical workers belies the general belief that what really distinguishes the present level of unemployment from any previous period is the number of white-collar redundancies. True, as unemployment has risen, so too have an increasing number of technical workers found their way to the Employment Exchange, but in nowhere near the numbers to justify current mythology. The first classification, giving the number of unemployed labourers shows that in the 1970s, just as in the 1930s, unemployment falls predominantly on the poorest workers.

A careful look at the data on the age distribution of the unemployed casts doubt on another current myth. If one ignores for the moment the percentage of men over 60 who are unemployed, then, as can be seen in the following table, the highest rates of unemployment are to be found amongst workers below the age of 30. Unemployment is not concentrated among older workers. In fact, the reverse is true and this is one of the more important characteristics to note about present unemployment. These men will be unemployed workers with young families.

Table 12: AGE DISTRIBUTION OF THE UNEMPLOYED

	July 1972		Changes in levels	
	Number (thousands)	% rate	(thousands)	% changes
Under 20	82.1	(7.4)	61.5	298
20 and under 40	275.0	(4.7)	168.1	157
40 and under 55	148.0	(3.5)	74.3	101
55 and under 60	53.4	(3.9)	105.3	166
60 and under 65	115.4	(9.8)		
65 and over	2.1	(0.5)	3.5	63
All ages	676.0	4.8	405.7	150

The last table in the section contains no surprises. It looks at the regional variations in unemployment in December 1971. The old-established landmarks are still there. Those regions which were characterized by high structural unemployment in the 1930s still bear these scars.

Table 13: REGIONAL VARIATIONS IN UNEMPLOYMENT
(DECEMBER 1971): NUMBERS REGISTERED AS
UNEMPLOYED EXPRESSED AS A PERCENTAGE
OF THE TOTAL NUMBER OF EMPLOYEES
(EMPLOYED AND UNEMPLOYED)

Region	Registered Unemployed % Men	Women
South East	3.2	0.8
East Anglia	4.5	1.4
East Midlands	4.6	1.3
South West	5.3	2.0
Yorkshire & Humberside	6.2	1.6
North West	6.5	1.9
Wales	6.6	2.8
West Midlands	7.1	1.6
Scotland	8.5	3.4
Great Britain	5.5	1.6
Northern Ireland	10.4	5.3

SOURCE: *Department of Employment Gazette* (HMSO, January 1972).

OLD-AGE PENSIONERS

The most detailed study on the poverty amongst old people is the
Financial and Other Circumstances of Retirement Pensioners.[9] The
report contains two pieces of information which are highly relevant

Table 14: RETIREMENT PENSIONERS WITH NO INCOME
APART FROM THE RETIREMENT PENSION
(AND NATIONAL ASSISTANCE) IN JUNE 1965

Age Group	Couples %	Single Men %	Single Women %	All Retirement Pensioners[†] %
60–64	–	–	20	20
65–69	9	22	27	16
70–74	11	24	31	20
75–79	15	22	41	27
80–84	21	31	42	34
85 and over	24	35	50	44

† The figure for all retirement pensioners is calculated with an adjustment
for non-response.
SOURCE: *Financial and Other Circumstances of Retirement Pensioners,*
Table II.4. Quoted from A. B. Atkinson, *Poverty in Britain and the Reform
of Social Security* (CUP, 1969).

to this section. The first is that in June 1965, one in five of all retired old people had no other income apart from their old-age pension and national assistance supplements. Table 14 gives a more detailed breakdown for this group.

The Ministry's inquiry also showed that 34 per cent of married couples, 40 per cent of single men and 62 per cent of single women had resources (before National Assistance) which were below the current National Assistance scale then in force. So nearly half of all retirement pensioners (47 per cent) were in a position where they would fall below the national minimum unless they applied for a means-tested addition to their pension. As Tony Atkinson sardonically notes, it can hardly be claimed as fulfilling the Beveridge objective of ensuring 'that every citizen, fulfilling during his working life the obligation of service according to his powers, can claim as of right when he is past work an income adequate to maintain him'.

In Section 2, we looked at those people living below the poverty-line. A very large number of these people were old-age pensioners who, without the help of a means-tested addition to the pension, had inadequate resources. Why, when additional financial help

Table 15: REASONS FOR NOT APPLYING FOR NATIONAL ASSISTANCE* (JUNE 1965)

Reasons for non-application†	Married Couples %	Proportion Single Men %	Single Women %
Lack of knowledge or misconception	37	34	35
'Managing all right'	20	30	38
Pride, dislike of charity, dislike of going to National Assistance Board	33	27	23

* The question was only put to those retirement pensioners apparently entitled to National Assistance.
† Some pensioners gave more than one reason and are counted twice.
SOURCE: *Financial and Other Circumstances of Retirement Pensioners*, Table III.21. Quoted from A. B. Atkinson, *Poverty in Britain and the Reform of Social Security* (CUP, 1969).

could be gained from 'The Assistance', did so many refuse to apply for it?

This was a question asked by research workers employed on the survey. Their answers are to be found in the table below. The two main reasons why old people eligible for assistance did not register their right to benefit were a lack of knowledge about entitlement and the stigma associated with means-tested help.

One-parent Families

Another cause of family poverty is the loss or absence of one of the parents. Just how poor many of these families are was illustrated by Dennis Marsden's study *Mothers Alone*.[10] His study, which was carried out in 1967, found that the average total income of the fatherless families in the sample was 123 per cent of the national assistance scale rate, or just over £9 a week to keep a mother and two children, paying a rent of £2 a week. But the National Assistance did not guarantee every mother a minimum income. 8 per cent of the families had incomes below 90 per cent of the scale rates.

Marsden's survey found that widows had relatively larger incomes. Unmarried, divorced and separated mothers with young, illegitimate children had the lowest incomes and, unlike widows who were eligible for National Insurance benefits, were most dependent on National Assistance for their income. Table 16 does something to bring this study up to date.

Table 16: NUMBER OF ONE-PARENT FAMILIES IN RECEIPT OF SUPPLEMENTARY BENEFIT SINCE 1968

	Thousands					Total one-parent families (including dependants)
Year	No.	Motherless families Dependants	No.	Fatherless families Dependants	Total Dependants	
1968	6	13	182	359	372	560
1969	5	12	199	386	397	602
1970	6	14	212	406	420	638
1971	7	17	238	464	481	726

source: DHSS Annual Special Sample Inquiries.

LONG-TERM SICK AND DISABLED

More than three million adults living at home in Britain are physically or mentally impaired and almost 1,250,000 of them are seriously handicapped. Between 35 per cent and 40 per cent of them receive supplementary benefits. They are on the whole poorer than the rest of the community, often housed inadequately and restricted in their educational and employment opportunities. *Handicapped and Impaired in Great Britain*[11] showed that about half of handicapped persons have incomes at or near the supplementary benefit level and their average income is less than half the national average.

This confirmed the findings of Sally Sainsbury's pilot study in 1965 of 211 persons registered as physically handicapped by the welfare departments of London, Essex and Middlesex.[12] Only 13 per cent of those interviewed were wage-earners and so the vast majority were dependent upon State benefits. Resources were limited, not only because the disabled person's income was low, but because savings were also low. Few had any capital assets and only 20 per cent had savings in excess of £100. The proportion of owner-occupiers in the sample was below the national average. Household income, too, tended to be below average income. There were three times as many people in the sample living below 140 per cent of the National Assistance Scale, as in the total population. Indeed, Sally Sainsbury found that more than half of the households included in the sample were dependent on benefits, while two-fifths of households which received no State benefits had total incomes of less than 140 per cent of the basic National Assistance Scale.

NOTES

1 B. S. Rowntree, *Poverty: A Study of Town Life* (Macmillan, 1901).

2 *Poverty: 10 Years After Beveridge* (PEP, 1952), p. 25.

3 See A. J. Harrison, *Low Pay and Child Poverty*, CPAG Discussion Papers 1, (1972).

4 A. B. Atkinson, *Poverty in Britain and the Reform of Social Security* (CUP, 1969), p. 74.

5 *Circumstances of Families* (HMSO, 1967), pp. 12–14.

6 *Administration of the Wage Stop* (HMSO, 1961), p. 6.

7 See Adrian Sinfield and Fred Twine, 'The Working Poor', *Poverty*, 12/13 (1969).

8 Stephen Winyard kindly reworked the official earnings data for me. He is also responsible for all the statistical information in the unemployment section.

9 HMSO, 1969.

10 Penguin Books, 1969.

11 HMSO, 1971.

12 Sally Sainsbury, *Registered Disabled* (Bell, 1970).

JEREMY SANDFORD

Britain's Gypsies and Travellers

Travellers is the best name for them. This word includes both the traditional Gypsy Romanies, and also those thousands who have joined them in their wandering way of life.

They are not treated well by us.

Members of Havering Council in Essex advocated using dogs to evict twelve Gypsy caravans from a public park.

Gypsies were eventually removed from Oldchurch Road in Romford after a battle with fifty police.

Epsom and Walton Downs conservators declared their intention of having security corps men to help the police repel the hundreds of Gypsy caravans visiting their traditional camping place on Epsom Downs, where they come the week before Derby day.

The Town Clerk of Epsom and Ewell said: 'The police have promised to co-operate to their utmost in obtaining the names and addresses of caravan owners before they can establish themselves on the Downs.'

People at Badger's Mount near Sevenoaks threatened to withhold their rates unless something was done about the 'nuisance' from Gypsies parked by the Orpington bypass.

At Caddington, near Luton, farmers with a tractor and a mechanical digger tried to remove a caravan family from their site. A farmer said: 'The village has been forced to live in filth since Gypsies moved in.' And a member of the Parish Council said: 'The Gypsies have been guilty of many flagrant acts of assault, even offering violence to a lady.'

Up to 200 Securicor men have been involved in evictions in the Midlands.

Gypsies have grown used to defining their relationship to society

75

in terms of its hostility to them. Society is apt to shrug off its duty to these people by saying : 'These of course are not real Gypsies. Your real Gypsy is clean, and has colourful and picturesque ways. These people are just layabouts, littering up our countryside and our roadsides.'

But as Norman Dodds has said : 'There are good Gypsies and bad Gypsies . . . whether they are good or bad they are all human beings.'

In a country lane in Breconshire two caravans are drawn up. Leafy trees arch overhead. A woman sits outside one caravan by a camp fire, squatting on her haunches in the slight drizzle. Ragged children play about her. She has been sitting, immobile, for the last two hours.

By a trunk road near London Airport, I find another two caravans parked. One of them has a rusty chassis which seems to be coming loose from its wheels. There is no glass in its gaping windows. Inside, on one fetid bed with blankets but no sheets, there are seven children asleep. The other bed sleeps the head of the family, his wife and his friend.

There are travellers in most British counties. Nearly half live in the South East. One fifth are in the West Midlands.

Other countries have more Gypsies than we have. Czechoslovakia and Bulgaria each have over 200,000 (respectively 1.5 per cent and 3 per cent of the population).

Hitler gassed 600,000 Gypsies.

Gypsies in many foreign countries have their own intricate and beautiful Gypsy lore. Britain's Gypsies, however, in my experience, do not keep up many of the old exotic customs of their forebears.

The most respected used to be those with most Romany (traditional Gypsy) blood. Now it is sometimes those with the flashiest caravans or the newest lorries who command the respect and, however pure his lineage, the 'abject Romany in his tent' may be despised.

The name Gypsy derives from a habit of the first Gypsies who came here from India; trying to give themselves status they claimed to come from 'Little Egypt'. It was thought that they had made the nails for Christ's cross and they carried letters, allegedly from the Pope, asking that they should be given free passage, since they were expiating this sin. Later, they were joined by others—families dispossessed during the enclosures and navvies who wandered round digging out the 'navigations' (canals) or building railways.

There are a third fewer old people in Gypsy households than in the population as a whole, perhaps because of the rigours of the Gypsy way of life. On the other hand, eleven per cent of Gypsy families include more than five children, compared with one per cent for the rest of the nation.

It is thought that about three-quarters of the traveller population has never lived in a house; most of them do not want to. Those Gypsies who have lived in houses and then return to the road usually give as their reason that they 'felt the call of the road'; in the case of only one in ten is the housing shortage given as a reason. Horse-drawn caravans are getting fairly rare now; there are only a hundred or so left, mostly in the north of England. At the most recent official census, some Gypsy families were found living in huts and hundreds of families in tents.

Although the number of Gypsies is growing, an increasingly over-crowded island seems to have less and less room for them. Their traditional stopping places are built over or surrounded by stakes, or they have great ravines dug across them by bulldozers, or mounds of earth erected round them.

Grattan Puxon, ex-secretary of the Gypsy Council, told me : 'In spite of government pressure, police still harass gypsies. It frequently happens that police tow travellers over the boundary into the next administrative area, and dump them there by the roadside. Then the people there will send their police to summons them, and tell them to move on.'

At one place travellers, towed on by police, dumped, picked up and towed on again, had at last settled down to have a meal—their first that day. There was a little girl there whose foot was in need of medical treatment. Her mother had made an appointment for her but feared that if they were moved on again she wouldn't be able to keep it. The child might become crippled. None the less the caravan was once again moved on by police.

The Caravan Sites Act 1968 specified that sites must be provided by local authorities for Gypsies in their areas. Later this was made compulsory. But many local authorities are still ignoring the ruling.

The story can be read in a succession of Government circulars.

In 1962, a circular said :

Moving people off one unauthorized site and leaving them to
find another is no solution, and no answer to the human and
social problems involved. These can only be resolved by the provision of proper sites, in which the caravan families can settle
down under decent conditions, and in reasonable security.

Authorities were urged to carry out local surveys, to inform the
Minister of the results and to take action to provide the necessary
caravan sites.

The results of the circular were disappointing. Only 37 of the 62
county councils in England and Wales reported either that a survey
on the lines suggested in the circular had been carried out, or that
investigations had been undertaken by the county planning officer
in association with the district and borough councils. Of these 37
councils, 13 concluded that new permanent sites were not needed
either because existing provision was adequate or because they considered that settlement did not offer a satisfactory solution to the
problem. If travellers were itinerant agricultural workers they did
not require permanent sites; if they were scrap-metal dealers they
would create fresh problems by destroying site amenities and littering the area with the debris of their trade.

In 1966 another Government circular stated :

The Minister of Housing and Local Government asks all County
Councils, and every County Borough, which had Gypsies in its
area at the time of the census [that was a census of the number
of Gypsies in Britain in March 1965], to send him a report in six
months' time of the action they may have taken, or propose, in
response to this circular. He hopes that by then plans will be well
advanced for the provision of at least one site in each county
affected. Meanwhile the Minister would ask that nothing should
be done to add needlessly to the difficulties of Gypsy households.

Local authorities acted sluggishly if at all; many did nothing. A
further Government circular of October 1967 said : 'The coming
winter is bound to bring considerable problems of unauthorized
camping in areas where no site provision has been made, despite the
requests made in the Minister's Circulars 6/62, 26/66 . . . Until

such sites are provided, the Minister and Secretary of State emphasize that the needless removing of one Gypsy family from one area to another should not take place.'

The harassing went on and another circular, in August 1968, said :

> The Ministers have repeatedly emphasized that Gypsies should not be needlessly moved on from place to place until sites have been provided for them. It is particularly important that Local Authorities should not drive Gypsies out of their areas, to become the responsibility of neighbouring authorities, in the period before a country-wide network of sites is established. Moving-on operations and the subsequent clearing, ditching, and fencing of land that has been used by Gypsies can be very expensive and by itself contributes nothing to the overall solution of the problem. Somewhat similar considerations apply where Local Authorities are considering the timing of planning enforcement action against travelling families who may have bought a plot of land and stationed a caravan on it without the necessary planning permission and site licence.
>
> In some circumstances it may be possible to defer enforcement action until sites have been established in the county into which such families could go if they wished.

But again there were many local authorities who failed to begin to build sites. A further circular of May 1970 stated : 'with the coming into operation of part II of the Caravan Sites Act 1968 the question before [Local Authorities] is not whether sites for Gypsy caravans should be established but where in the areas they should be?' It went on to speak of possible objections to such sites : 'the Minister trusts that authorities will adopt effective means to dispel any signs of apprehension about the likely effect of providing controlled sites.'

In the face of continuing resistance from local authorities, Gypsies have been fighting increasingly steadfast battles for their rights. One of the first of these battles was at St Mary Cray where, after attempts to evict them, thirty families barricaded themselves in, defending themselves with five-foot railway lines embedded in concrete. There was much fighting, and at least five attempts were

made to remove them. Later the Police Federation urged that
police should not be actively involved in these scenes. The final
result of all this was that the local authority provided a site for
them, and has also found them work. Gypsies have been given the
job of collecting all the abandoned cars in the area. They are breaking up a vast dump of 7,000 cars and selling them—an arrange-
ment profitable to Bromley Borough Council and also to the Gypsies
themselves.

The next council to provide a site was Havering. This was after
another heroic stand by the Gypsies on Hornchurch Airfield.

A fine stand at Eastern Avenue, Redbridge followed, and a
permanent site has now been made at Forest Road.

At Hillingdon the council was employing a full-time 'ranger'
whose job it was to move on the Gypsies. It is said that the council
was planning to take on a second ranger. There were about eighty
families here. After being harassed by rangers, many families moved
on to a site called Coln Park Caravan Site, at West Drayton. The
response of the council was to send in towing vehicles, bulldozers
and police. But the travellers received a tip-off, and barricaded the
gate. The council got a bulldozer to smash down the gate. A caravan
was brought up to the gate and set on fire. Behind this, a second
caravan was filled with concrete and made immovable. Chaos followed. But the result was that Hillingdon also agreed to provide a
site.

At Enfield there had always been a stopping place. Recently the
council decided to close it down. Fifteen families moved their
caravans into Mollison Avenue. The council arrived with towing
vehicles, but the Gypsies talked to the workmen, who said they were
not happy about this and would refer it to their union, the NUP.
The union decided that no force must be used. So the Gypsy women
roped themselves to the drawbars of their vehicles. The towing
vehicle backed up to the caravans, the workmen refused to go
further, the women clung to the tow-bar. . . . At this point a
councillor announced that he would meet a delegation of families
if they were prepared to leave voluntarily. The Gypsies agreed,
and left. Next day they asked to see the councillor, but he seemed
to have changed his mind. 'No, I didn't mean leave the site, I
meant leave the borough. Anyway, I don't speak with Gypsies.'
The families moved to Alma Road, from which they were also

evicted, so they went on again to some waste land near Turkey Street. It was at that point that this council, too, said it was considering giving the Gypsies a permanent site.

I went to St Mary Cray, near Orpington, with its vast pile of cars surrounded by trees. Cars were piled high up into the sky, some rusty, some still brightly painted, some crushed into fragments, some still whole. Between the bodies of the cars children played constantly through this bizarre playground. The council site, surrounded by wire mesh which now has holes in it, has hard concrete standing for twelve caravans. Each caravan has a washhouse, complete with shower and washbasin.

A man here said : 'This is a good site. Placid and tranquil. This is all I want, I wouldn't want more. The only thing is, some people here take advantage. They burned down one of the council trailers last night.'

Mrs Luis Devall said : 'I like it here, it's nice, but I still remember the old days sometimes. When we used to be in the old horse wagons, and we'd pull 'em alongside a meadow in the evening and poove (graze) the horses in the grass of the meadow, and in the morning we'd be gone on again.'

Until recently a score of Gypsy families lived in an urban encampment at the Culverts, Battersea, situated inside the narrow triangle formed by three railways and approachable only through a dark arch or along a footbridge. Some lived in houses and some in caravans. Every single couple there I talked to had met while 'hopping'. Most of them were Gypsies, whether they lived in caravans or houses. As they claimed, this must have been Britain's most metropolitan camp site, and its population was probably closest to being 'integrated' with the rest of the population.

'There's been four generations of my family here,' said Barbara Mills. 'Think of the old song :

> She slept all night in a tinker's arms,
> Among the wheat and straw—

'Gypsies may move to houses but soon the old travelling urge comes out in them. My nephew was in a house, he was well set up. But when the urge came on him, he sold up and went hopping. Still we get the urge as the summer comes. Gypsies want to get away. They're independent. They want to get away.'

Against the railway arches stood a flower-seller's cart and a half-made caravan. The Romany who made it, Jimmy Penfold, said :

'In the old days, Romanies used to put a floor down and do step-dancing. In those days Rom married Rom. They'd marry each other because they were always travelling around so that's how they did their courting. Then they'd go off bundling (that is, with a bundle on their backs), and a bit later they'd get themselves a varda. And they didn't have birth certificates then. They had the Family Bible, that they wrote their names in.'

Some interesting information is contained in a document called *Gypsies and Other Travellers*, compiled by the Sociological Research Section of the Ministry of Housing and Local Government (HMSO, 1967). 'The dictionary definition of Gypsy,' says the Report, 'is a member of a wandering race of Indian origin; a Romany.' Although the term has primarily an ethnic meaning, it is often used loosely for all the people described in the report, whether 'true Romanies' or not. Since a recent High Court ruling a Gypsy is defined, for legal purposes, as a person without a fixed abode who leads a nomadic life dwelling in tents or other shelters or caravans or other vehicles; i.e., as a class of person and not a member of a particular race.

In a foreword to the document, the then Housing Minister, Anthony Greenwood, wrote :

The world around [the Gypsies] has altered so rapidly that their roving life can no longer be carried on without hardship—indeed the report reminds us of the remarkable fact that for most traveller families there is nowhere they can legally put their home; they are within the law only when moving along the road. The travellers' way of life and their attitude to amenities in both town and country clash with those of most other people. House-dwellers often find that unlawful encampments are a squalid nuisance. The fact that many travellers are illiterate adds to their difficulties in a complex and increasingly urbanized society, and limits their understanding of a more settled way of life. The children are apt to suffer most.

But all too often the settled community is concerned chiefly to persuade or even force the Gypsy families to move on over the boundary to the next district or the neighbouring county.

The move-on policy employed by local authorities can be well seen in a recent controversy between Aldridge-Brownhills Council and Birmingham Corporation. Mr Nicholls, Clerk of the Council, said, 'Birmingham carry out this ruthless action of evicting tinkers and then get their bailiffs to dump them in our territory. They have been dumped in some of our beauty spots. Birmingham has provided quite a large sum of money for a temporary site for Gypsies, but that doesn't excuse this very unneighbourly gesture.'

The Ministry report goes on :

. . . After the war the travellers' greatest difficulty was to find somewhere where he could camp in peace. He was increasingly being made to leave his traditional camping places, some of which were being developed, while others were simply being barred to him. He was not told where he could legitimately go, and the remaining camping places were becoming increasingly crowded. It seemed to him that only when he was on the move was he safe from the law; when he stopped, he was breaking it. But his reasons for constant travelling were declining. He was beginning to want his children to go to school. The demand for traditional Gypsy craft work was diminishing and increasingly the traveller was turning to new ways of making a living which did not require constant travelling. In increasing numbers travellers were turning to scrap metal dealing.

It was perhaps on this latter point that the objections of the settled population were centred. They complained that unsightly scrap metal was littered wherever the travellers camped, and that their domestic litter was a danger to health; that they used the fields as lavatories and were generally dirty; that they begged water from householders and intimidated those not giving it readily; that they littered the hedges with drying washing; that they allowed their horses to destroy crops and were not averse to stealing. Their strongest critics considered them social parasites.

As regards numbers, the report estimated about 15,000 Gypsies in England and Wales, but said it felt that this was an underestimate. Adding the figures for Scotland and Ireland and allowing for this underestimation brings the figure, according to my reckoning, to about 25,000 Gypsies in the British Isles as a whole living in caravans at the moment.

The surveyors carried out various interviews, and a number of the travellers interviewed said that they had, at some time, lived in houses. There are also, of course, many travellers who, for one reason or another, are at present living in houses. They think of themselves as travellers and might take to the road again if conditions became less appalling. So that the number 50,000 might give us a true estimate of those who would actually claim to be Gypsies in Britain; many of these would like to be on the road if we Gorgios could behave in a reasonable way towards them.

The report continues :

The first reference to them in Britain dates from 1505 (an entry on the accounts of the Lord High Treasurer for Scotland); but they had no doubt crossed over well before then. Although they adopted characteristics from each country through which they passed, they carried with them the language, customs, and occupations of the low caste Indian tribes from which they sprang and which still survive in a much-modified form to this day.

Their traditional occupations followed closely those which were cursed, or prohibited to upper castes in ancient India—including fortune-telling; horse training and dealing, smithery; and entertainment by singing, dancing, playing musical instruments, acting, juggling and acrobatics. In particular, horse dealing for men and fortune-telling for women were among the occupations of the first Gypsies to arrive in Britain. The immigrants also became noted for their wood carving, from which developed crafts such as peg making, chair mending, and flower making. The Gypsies' occupations were suited to their nomadic life and in the early days they travelled on pack-horses or with horse-drawn trollies, and camped in tents. It was not until the early nineteenth century that they adopted the covered living wagon.

In the period following their arrival in Great Britain, the Gypsies, or 'Egyptians' as they called themselves, travelled in large bands causing consternation among the settled population. Repressive legislation was enacted in 1530, 1554 and 1562 and the latter Acts made all immigrant adult 'Egyptians' and others found in their company liable to be treated as felons, to have their goods forfeited, and to be put to death. At York in 1596, 106 Gypsies were condemned to death at one sitting of the Quarter Sessions, but most were later reprieved for the sake of their children. Repressive treatment of the Gypsies continued throughout the seventeenth and eighteenth centuries but the first Act repealing the earlier legislation was passed in 1783. The romantic and philanthropic interest in the Gypsy way of life engendered by George Borrow and others in the nineteenth century, culminating in the founding of the Gypsy Lore Society in 1888, helped to ease their existence. Gypsies are, however, still singled out as a class in modern legislation.

. . . Though none of the travellers included in the survey lived in houses, there were very few who lived in the traditional Gypsy caravan. The horse-drawn living wagon with its association of traditional Romany life is now fast disappearing and 95 per cent of families recorded in the census had trailer caravans, designed to be towed behind a car or lorry. 188, or a mere 6 per cent of all traveller families still had a horse-drawn wagon as their home. Rather more families whose accommodation was recorded possessed huts and a few had tents, almost always as additional living quarters.

. . . Ever since the sixteenth century there has been legislation which is inimical to the Gypsy way of life. More recently the Public Health Act 1936, the Town and Country Planning Act 1947 (now consolidated in the Act of 1962), the Highways Act 1959 and the Caravan Sites and Control of Development Act 1960 have all been used to prevent travellers from setting up camps. Unless either the authorities turn a blind eye to casual traveller encampments, or authorized encampments are made available within the terms of the 1936 Act, the traveller can never find a secure stopping place, except in the limited circumstances which are exempt from the Act. This amounts to the virtual outlawing of his way of life.

The Gypsy Council has put this more forcibly in evidence they submitted to the compilers of the HMSO document:

Sometimes we just stop somewhere in the morning to have breakfast. The police come along and make us move on; they take us to the end of the beat and there is another lot waiting for us who take us to the end of their beat and so it goes on till we are run into the next county. At times like that we can't make a living;

we can't wash; we get no chance even to cook and eat. This is
hell on earth; the worse kind of police state and not at all the
sort of fair play Englishmen like to brag about. This has nothing
to do with Green Belts or a planned economy or any of the other
good news Government policies which we agree must limit freedom to a certain extent; it is just a case of plain cussedness, in-
tolerance and perhaps thoughtlessness.

The kind of action which local authorities reported they had used
to remove travellers from unauthorized places, extended from 'informal' warnings to the physical removal of their vans on to the
roadway. Among the reported methods of keeping them off these
places were the fixing of posts, trenching, the dumping of gravel
across the entrance to the land, or the ploughing up of the land to
make it unsuitable for camping. Private owners sometimes take
similar action, and a case was reported of the ground being churned
up with a heavy tractor.

Where the travellers were camped on publicly owned land, the
most common form of prevention reported was informal persuasion
to leave the unauthorized places by public health inspectors and
police, often in collaboration. This was sometimes done after a 'per-
mitted stay' had expired or as soon as the travellers' presence in the
area was known. One reporting officer spoke of a 'merry-go-round,
chasing them over our borders and from site to site within our area'.
Apart from the simple eviction of trespassers from council land,
where the powers used were detailed, this action had usually been
taken as enforcement of section 124 of the Highways Act 1959, or
of the statutory nuisance provisions of the Public Health Act 1936.
Enforcement notices and discontinuance orders under the Town and
Country Planning Act 1962 were also used in attempts to end un-
authorized camping. Camping on commons is regulated to Common
Schemes set up under the Commons Act 1899, or by orders issued
under section 23 of the Caravan Sites and Control Department Act
1960. Some authorities have powers to regulate the stationing of
caravans within their area under local Acts, such as the West Riding
County Council (General Powers) Act 1951, though many local Act
powers were repealed and replaced by the 1960 Act.

The use of private land for stationing caravans is now regulated
by the Town and Country Planning Act 1962 and the Caravan
Sites and Control of Development Act 1960, and this has severely

curtailed the number of places available to travellers. When un-authorized and unlicensed sites are used, the local authority has to take enforcing action against the owner or occupier of the land, rather than the caravan occupiers, even when the caravans are stationed on the land against the owner's wishes. In the cases reported, the owner or occupier was often warned informally before any notices were served, and the authority sometimes gave assistance in the removal of the unwanted caravans. One case was reported of a traveller who was fined a total of £313 plus costs for parking his two caravans on his own land for which planning permission had been refused. In some cases where the families were employed as seasonal workers, the local authority encouraged or enforced their removal as soon as their employment ceased.

I quote from the report again :

Many authorities have a general policy towards travellers' un-authorized camping. Some discourage caravans on any unauthor-ized places within their area. One county borough always sends a constable to give 2–3 hours' notice to quit; others give longer notice—a day, 48 hours, a week, or at most, a fortnight. One borough council, under a local Act, has given approval to the stationing of caravans only twice in the past ten years, following requests from the midwifery service. Another borough appointed a 'caravan removal and general duties officer' who was reported to have succeeded in removing twenty caravans a month.

. . . As many as 60 per cent of all the families found on un-licensed camping places and on the verge of roads or lanes were on sites where the authorities reported having taken action at some time (not necessarily recently) to prevent the use of the site.

. . . It is difficult for the house-dweller fully to realize the trau-matic nature of these enforced moves.

The famous eviction of the Gypsies from Darenth Woods in Kent was described by Patrick O'Donovan in *The Observer* a few years ago.

The Gypsies were routed today in Darenth Woods. The planning committee of Dartford Rural Council won. By the end of the day the woods looked like the site of some vicious World War I en-counter. It was a peaceful victory, but it was not a famous one.

The Gypsies have used these woods, mostly for winter quarters for five years. There is a heavy concentration of them in Kent, largely because the myriads of small intensive farms demand casual labour in the season.

Two thousand of them used to winter in Belvedere Marshes, in Corke's Meadow and on Barden's Lane Farm, all in this part of England. But these have been closed. So 98 families of them were this morning living in Darenth Woods—which of course are not their property.

The council has used bulldozers to build a shabby rampart of earth and roots round part of the wood to stop more Gypsies getting in.

Their family names are King and Lee and Smith and they live scattered through the woods in tight groups. Some live in the old painted rococo caravans, some in smart new trailers and some in home-made boxes on wheels.

They live by casual labour in spring and summer and in winter by grinding knives, collecting rags and scrap, by selling artificial flowers and clothes pegs, and, according to the locals, by less respectable means. They have been buying their water lately at one shilling a churn.

They were due to leave at 8.30 this morning. There was a smell of wood smoke. Dogs and cats played round the wheels, and horses—the best-cared for things in the woods—ate the fresh hay, but no preparations to move seemed to have been made.

Mr Norman Dodds, Labour MP for Erith and Crayford, stood by his caravan where he had spent the night. He has made the Gypsy cause his. He is a sturdy, plain-spoken man. He can have no political motive in this. His campaigning will do him no good politically. He just likes Gypsies and believes their treatment in England the worst in Europe.

At 9.20 the forces of Dartford Rural Council arrived, a loud and faintly menacing procession of tractors and lorries. The drivers looked embarrassed and the employees in the lorries were silent.

The chief superintendent of the police from Gravesend was there, an avuncular figure who went from family to family asking them to move as a favour and offering to help. He and a few officers with him behaved as the police behave on the 'Come to Britain' posters. His distaste for his job was obvious. The men from the council hitched up the caravans and wagons and began to tow them out of the mud.

At 9.50 the first lot was on the move—an old flat farm wagon and a delivery trap—both horse drawn—but now dragged ignominiously away behind a lorry. One by one the caravans were hauled out of the wood and away down the muddy lane that leads down the hill. Engines revved, bonfires blazed with rubbish, children screamed with excitement and the Gypsies did almost all they could to help.

They were polite, even deferential. Only one man shouted before he went that they were mad to move. Their gentleness was partly due to Mr Dodd's advice and the prudence of the police. Even more, it was due to the fact that they are used to this sort of thing. Gypsies don't fight back in public.

One huge old lady in a tent-like cardigan fastened with a crown piece asked me; 'All right to burn that hut, sir? We can't move it. Used it four and a half years. Seems a shame.' She had no idea where she was going. She had no pity for herself.

One by one the caravans moved off, horses were harnessed, tractors heaved, old bicycles, prams and bedsteads were thrown on to the trucks. And they were all taken a mile or two away to the main A2 road. They are being allowed to stop there on the grass verge—until Monday. After that no one has any idea at all what to do with them. They are no one's responsibility and no one wants them.

The eviction was a victory for Mr Leslie Reeves, chairman of Dartford Rural Council planning committee. He has fought a brilliant little campaign to achieve this. He thinks it unfair that the Gypsies should be his council's responsibility. Mr Dodds wanted them left another ten weeks until the casual worktime started again.

Dr Hill, Minister of Housing and Local Government, has asked councils throughout the country to do something. The empty hospital and its grounds were refused to Gypsies. The Government insists that they are and must remain a local responsibility.

No doubt some of the Gypsies themselves would like a house or a flat and the luxury of a factory job. Their difficulty is how to start getting both these things. The children have been going to school in Darenth and they resented weekends because it interfered with the pleasure of such an ordered life. The headmaster—with the vicar—is amongst the most urgent protesters against this move.

Mr Dodds would, if he could, find them permanent sites with water and sanitation as is done on the Continent. This would at least mean a steady education for the children and then in time the Gypsy 'problem' would disappear.

Tonight they have lit fires, put up their aerials and tethered their horses beside the traffic on the A2. They are not too worried about the future. After all they have been treated like this since Henry VIII's Parliament passed an Act 'Concerning Egyptians'.

'A roadside site where Gypsies squatted for six months was "abounding in rubbish and filth", the High Court was told yesterday.'

This sentence appeared in *The Guardian* in 1970. The average reader probably hardly stops to think about it but in such a brief sentence there often lies concealed a tragedy. The word 'squatted' should also have been in quotes, for Gypsies, after all, used to be able to park more or less where they liked on our grass verges.

The period around 1900, they say, was a happy time for them. Then, so they claim, a tolerant nation was ready to allow them to camp beside the highways and ready also to draw on their services for the various occasions when their labour was needed.

We still draw on their services. Whenever a concentrated work-force is needed—whether it be in hopping, potato picking, fruit picking, or road making, there you usually find the Gypsies. But the nation as a whole no longer seems to feel that it is right for them to have free stopping places. And the greatest enemy of all for the Gypsies has been the road widening which has done away with so many grass verges. Where verges remain, local authorities have gone so far as to dump rubbish, ash, bricks, or raise mounds on them, often in themselves very unsightly, in order to prevent the travellers using them in the way that they used to. Moreover, most of the commons on which they were traditionally able to stop have now been closed to them by an increasingly unpermissive and standardized society.

By 3 October, 1970, local authorities had said that they would provide sites for about half Britain's Gypsy population. This was a poor enough contribution. But, even if a Gypsy can get onto a site and even if the sites are completed within a reasonable period, the sites themselves are often highly unsuitable.

Too often the local authority sites have oppressive rules. A local authority that has provided a site is also given greater powers to harass Gypsies not lucky enough to get on one. Often surrounded by tall iron-mesh fences, these sites can remind one of America's Indian reservations, the last jest of a settled community that perhaps secretly envies the Gypsies their don't-care existence. Open-air fires are often forbidden, together with the erection of tents, the keeping of most animals and the accommodation of scrap. The traditional life style thus becomes impossible and this may have the effect of forcing Gypsies finally to give up their old self-sufficient ways, forcing them fairly and squarely on to Social Security. Is this what we want?

Travellers get so used to the hostility of society that they are suspicious of goodwill even when it is shown them. When a local authority site was provided at Llanelly, Gypsies didn't believe in it, even on its day of opening. They sent a small reconnaissance party to spy out whether it was anything like what they had been told.

All too often, people still think in terms of 'integrating the Gypsies into society'. A member of the Hertfordshire Liberals said : 'There's still forty-five Gypsy families roaming the countryside. The sooner Gypsy children can be sent to school, the sooner they can be integrated into society.' What would happen, I wonder, if with similar zeal travellers tried to integrate Gorgios into their society !

A dangerously patronizing attitude is also shown, I believe, by the missionary who told me : 'My job was to go all over the country on a bicycle, call on the camps, and persuade them to join the army. To give up making clothes pegs, to come out of the lanes and the byways, come out into the daylight, come out of the old smoky lanes, and get themselves so they were recognized by the country.'

The Housing Manager of Andover, in Hampshire, evolved a scheme of 'integrating' Gypsies into council houses. Twenty-four Gorgio inhabitants of Mylen Road, however, petitioned against this. 'We are discriminating not against blacks but against whites,' they said. 'Although the Gypsies may look black because they don't wash.' The council, however, were proof against this. 'The petition,' they said, 'has been received, noted—and ignored.'

To a certain extent the dislike of traveller caravanners rubs off on Gorgio caravans as well.

Mr Whiteman, editor of the magazine *Caravan*, in a paper which he presented to the Royal Society of Arts, put forward the interesting theory that the caravan evokes a racial memory not only in the people who participate in caravanning but in the people who oppose it—a racial memory which stems from the fear of dangerous barbarism and which has come to be associated with the nomad.

Despite this, an increasing number of Gorgios have learned the joys of living in a caravan. In a recent year it was revealed that about 35,000 Gorgios own their own caravans and tow them around. There are about 200,000 resident caravanners in all (excluding travellers) and no less than three million people who spend their holidays in a rented stationary caravan near some beauty spot or resort. The British caravan industry is the second largest in the world.

Thus, the Gorgio in his caravan either steals from the Gypsy his traditions—or persecutes him. Our attitude to the Gypsies can be compared with that of the Americans to their Indians. Americans have adopted many Indian customs and traditions—and they have largely destroyed them. We have taken from our Gypsies not only the caravans but also the traditional dress, the fairs and race meetings which Gypsies claim to have originated.

Local authorities nearly always seem to oppose caravan living on principle. But in a world of vast housing lists and something like three million people in inadequate housing, the caravan could offer a home to many which would be superior to what they have now.

About half of those 200,000 Gorgios living in caravans are there because they actually prefer it. They give roughly the same reasons as do the Gypsies. Gorgios I have spoken to give as their main reasons for living in a caravan the fresh air, the healthier life and a feeling that they are in closer contact with nature. Others speak of the cheapness and labour-saving quality of a caravan and point to the greater feeling of community to be found on a caravan site.

Most Gorgio caravan residents don't move around. But there is a significant proportion of Gorgios who use caravans exactly as travellers do, to move their homes to areas where there is work. Members of the Forces, those who build pipe-lines or lay electricity grids or motorways, and many others, seem increasingly to be taking up Gypsy-style living.

Extracts from a 'Newsletter' sent to the inmates of a Gorgio site near Farnborough state :

It must be realized by certain licencees that the accumulation of rubbish, old bicycles, scooters, etc. on the rear of bases must be cleared. Your store shed is supplied and further accumulation outside will not and never has been allowed.

Many bases, on inspection, are found in need of a general brushing off, especially under the caravan in question. Also some fences of gardens are still very untidy and not cared for. Please note it is time these offenders cleaned up and got their places in order.

I know it has been said that the company does not hesitate to evict anyone at the first opportunity; our older residents will know how untrue this statement is, but at the same time, let me make it quite clear that as a company we pursue a very straight policy and should any licensee need to be corrected or put in place this will be done, and should it ever become necessary to carry out an unsavoury task, such as eviction, the company will not hesitate to do so.

One paragraph at least in this newsletter might have been more kindly conveyed through personal contact. It says :

People living alone. In my last letter I stressed the need of all of you living alone to register at the Warden's office the address of your nearest relative or someone who may be approached should occasion ever arise that you may be in need of help. Note—the company cannot hold itself responsible for you in case of illness or perhaps having to arrange things for you.

The treatment of Gypsies, however, is far worse than that.

The Gypsies have so far been unorganized. Their thought patterns, language and customs are different from those of Gorgios. For example, they find it hard to understand what is going on at the Gorgio law courts. Their culture is so far from ours that the only way to secure true justice when a traveller goes to court would be to have an interpreter of some sort, as is done when non-English-speaking people are brought to trial.

D

Gordon Boswell, in the *Book of Boswell* (Gollancz, 1970), describes well the difficulties of a traveller in court:

> The Gypsy never says nothing until he's prosecuted, and then he rears up and tries to defend himself—very hasty, very sharp, very sweet. He's only got a few seconds to do it. He loses his temper and he says what he thinks in his uneducated way. If he would have the patience to talk to these people, but without education it can't be put over. The show can't be put over where it comes to prosecution and defence. Against—that is—the educated man.

The need for organization amongst travellers was the subject of an address by Gordan Boswell at the most important meeting place for travellers—Appleby Fair.

Speaking from a loud-speaker van at this great gathering, he said:

> I'm not an educated man, but I'm a man of experience and I do know the way these things are done. Some of us have been talking this over—the travelling people who are on this ground—and we say and agree that we're willing to form this Travelling Traders' Association (suppose that will be the name). You may not see results right away, the first year . . . but there's got to be a beginning for all things, and this would be a great opportunity. Because you are driven from pillar to post, out of one district to another and you have no rest on the road. There is a remedy for our people, we are British subjects; we are entitled to justice. Other minorities in this country, even those who come from abroad, are looked after and their human rights respected, but you've got nothing, or nobody to care, or no place to live, nor even to rest. You are technically a people 'of no fixed abode' . . . and what I would like to see is some camps up and down the country. I'd like to see three types; a permanent camp where old people can go and stop and rest and be left in peace; a transit camp where you can come from one town to another and pay to go in and travel the country from north to south if you wish, and camps where you can stop in decent comfortable conditions in the winter months . . . I'm not thinking about you men. I'm I'm thinking about your little children. The time has come when they should all be able to go to school and get some education.

As has been shown, many Local Authorities have proved themselves amazingly slow at implementing what is now in fact the law
of the country. All sorts of excuses have been proffered.

Also important is the fact that, if they go away for long, travellers
may lose their place on the sites. Travellers traditionally go away to
work in those parts of the country where there is harvesting, fruit-
ing, and so on. Such travellers have sometimes been told on their
return to council sites that they have been away longer than the
statutory period and hence cannot return.

Gordon Boswell mentioned the permanent sites for those Gypsies
who wanted to settle down, the transit sites which should be
scattered around presumably a day's journey apart, and the winter
sites. The Government, at the moment, is only recommending the
first of these, and fewer than forty have been completed, of the
hundreds needed.

The allegation that Gypsies make a mess was discussed in an
article by John Seymour in *The Listener* (6 February, 1969). He
said :

Gypsies allegedly make a mess. But who makes the greater mess
—the Gypsy with his few old rags, scrapped motor-cars which
were lying around before he got there anyway, and his broken
prams, or the settled people with their deforestation, ribbon-
development, vast, hideous suburbs, and their bulldozer attitude
to the countryside? The real reason for the hatred of the nomad
is that some people cannot stand anybody who is different from
themselves.

And Richard Wade has said :

Has anyone ever tried to look at it from the other point of view?
The Gypsies are accused of being thieves, for instance, but to the
Gypsy mind we have stolen the countryside from him. He once
had wide grass verges at the sides of the roads to camp on and
nobody needed to interfere with him. There were enormous
commons where he could lose himself, and camp comfortably for
the winter without being moved on. All these have been closed,
taken away from him, by a land-hungry settled population which
in its greed seems to want everything the good Lord made.

Legislation has recently been passed to provide sites up and
down the country where Gypsies can stay, and thereafter nobody

will be allowed to camp by the side of the road any more, not even for a day. But the Gypsies themselves (whom no one so far has bothered to consult) think that left alone they could solve their own problem. Adjust the planning laws so that, with certain safeguards, a man can buy a suitable field and live on it with his trailer caravans when he is not travelling, and the 'Gypsy problem' will disappear.

There is no sign of this sensible idea being implemented. And we must ask, where does the future lie for travellers? In a world that increasingly seems bent on depriving them of their traditional way of life, who is to stand up for them?

Little seems to have resulted from Gordon Boswell's Travellers' Trading Association. Besides this there is the Gypsy Council which does not enjoy the full confidence of all travellers. Those Gypsies who dislike the government sites feel that the Gypsy Council was responsible for them.

Organizations and the thought patterns that go with them are alien to travellers. The Gypsy Council, consisting of Gypsies and their Gorgio advisers, runs an emergency service and is prepared to leave at an instant's notice to lend support to Gypsies in danger of eviction anywhere in Britain. The prompt action of Council members and their knowledge of the law have done an immense amount for Britain's travellers, both in giving on-the-spot help and also in bringing their plight to the public's attention.

A member of the Gypsy Council who has worked tirelessly for the travellers is George Marriott, a paralyzed ex-soldier and prisoner of war. He says, 'I got used to fighting the Gestapo in Germany. Now that I'm back I find that the Gestapo is here as well, in the form of police who, acting under orders, harry Gypsies and move them on. I fight them.'

Then there is the National Gypsy Education Council. This organization aims to bring education to Gypsy children, most of whom do not go to school at present. At Manchester, recently, where the students threw open their campus to the Gypsies, it was found that ninety per cent of the Gypsies could not read or write. The Advisory Committee for the Education of Romanies and other Travellers has as chairman Lady Plowden. And there is a breakaway pressure group of Gypsies—the Romany Guild.

Throughout Britain, Gypsy liaison groups have sprung up. Their aim is to form a needed connection between Gypsy ways of thought and local authorities, and to help local authorities set up sites which will be suitable for Gypsies. There is still a great need for people to undertake this important work. The Minister of Housing has, in a recent circular, suggested that local authorities should co-operate with such groups.

But the prospect for the future is still not a happy one. In a recent survey in one county it was discovered that a quarter of travellers would like to live in houses. Another quarter would like to live in their caravans but remain stationary. Half, however, want to continue to wander. It is for these, so far, that little provision has been made, and it seems that their life may become more rather than less complicated when, if ever, local authorities fulfil their statutory obligations to provide sites.

We continue to harass them. And yet the travellers' way of life conforms to what many Christians and others have throughout the ages aspired to. What mystics, prophets and holy men have been, they are. Like Christ, they think little of property, choose a simple way of life and take small thought for the morrow.

BOOKS AND JOURNALS FOR FURTHER READING

Boswell, Gordon, *The Book of Boswell* (Gollancz, 1970).

Clébert, Jean-Paul, trans. Charles Duff, *The Gypsies* (Vista Books, 1963). Mainly about foreign Gypsies.

Farre, Rowena, *A Time from the World* (Hutchinson, 1962).

Puxon, Grattan and Kenrick, Donald, *The Destiny of Europe's Gypsies* (Gollancz, 1972).

Puxon, Grattan, *On the Road* (National Council for Civil Liberties, 1968).

Sandford, Jeremy, *Gypsies* (Secker & Warburg, 1973).

Webb, G. E. C., *Gypsies: The Secret People* (London, 1960).

Gypsies and Other Travellers (HMSO, 1967).

Scotland's Travelling People (HMSO, 1971).

The Shadow on the Cheese: Notes on Gypsy Education (The National Gypsy Education Council, 1972).

Journal of the Gypsy Lore Society, c/o The University Library, Liverpool.

National Gypsy Education Council Newsletter, 204 Church Road,
Hanwell, London, W.5.
Romano Drom ('The Gypsy Newspaper'), c/o Vine Cottage, 53
Battersea Church Road, London, SW 11.

ORGANIZATIONS

The Gypsy Council, 61 Blenheim Crescent, London, W.11.
The Gypsy Lore Society, c/o Miss D. Yates, Hon. Sec., University
Library, Liverpool.
The National Gypsy Education Council, 61 Blenheim Crescent,
London, W.11.
The Advisory Committee for the Education of Romanies and other
Travellers, 204 Church Road, Hanwell, London, W.5.
The Romany Guild, Folly Lane Gypsy Caravan Site, London, E.17.
Romanestan Publications, c/o Tom Acton, Nuffield College, Oxford.
For all books about Gypsies.

PAUL HUNT

Disablement

'As a society Britain has what amounts to an elaborate system of discrimination against the disabled. We do not ensure that they have good housing, adequate community services, employment with dignity, or an adequate income.' Professor Peter Townsend came to this depressing conclusion in 1967 after reviewing the evidence of a survey carried out under his direction.[1] Similar conclusions have been reached by others who have studied the subject or who have conducted investigations in recent years. There may be arguments about some details of the situation, and about how it should best be tackled. But there is no disputing the fact that people who are physically (or mentally) handicapped in Britain today often do not get the help they ought to receive in a just and humane society.

Before attempting to show some of the major difficulties, particularly financial, besetting the disabled, the questions of definition and of incidence must be touched on. The blanket term 'the disabled' is often used to cover a great variety of conditions and degrees of handicap, both physical and mental. I shall have particularly in mind, however, young or middle-aged people whose capacity to perform the ordinary functions of daily living has been seriously impaired, for example by accidents or by conditions such as rheumatoid arthritis, multiple sclerosis, cerebral palsy, the after effects of polio, heart disease or strokes. It is true that this loosely defined group constitutes a minority *within* a minority. Many of the disabled find that their condition is not serious enough to be more than a nuisance. Of those who *are* substantially impaired, a majority are elderly, or mentally handicapped, or suffer from complete or partial blindness or deafness, or conditions such as epilepsy and chronic bronchitis. While there is certainly no intention to imply

that their situation, and particularly that of the mentally disabled
and the elderly, is any less important or less in need of action, I have
three main reasons for concentrating on the particular sub-group
described. Firstly, I am most familiar with their circumstances.
Secondly, it is largely they who feature in the publicity currently
given to the disabled. And thirdly, focusing primarily on one group
in this way helps to illustrate more clearly in the space available
some of the main issues involved in the whole complicated field of
disablement.

Until a national survey was started for the Department of Health
and Social Security in 1968, nobody had troubled to investigate the
numbers of people with disabilities in this country. Part of the difficulty has been that there is no generally accepted definition of
disability or handicap, and estimates of the numbers involved vary
enormously according to which definition is adopted. It has been
suggested, for instance, that at any one time in Britain there might
be only about 85,000 people who use wheelchairs, and many of
these may not be completely chair-bound.[2] Professor Townsend
calculated that there were in 1967 very roughly a million and a half,
or 3 per cent of the population, in groups *officially* described as
physically or mentally disabled.[3] The Government survey, the first
two volumes of which were published in May 1971,[4] estimated that
there were about 3 million people in Britain (excluding children
and those in institutions) with some physical, mental or sensory
impairment. Of these, one and a quarter million were defined as
'very severely, severely, or appreciably, handicapped'.[5] Estimates and
surveys in other countries have produced figures of 6 per cent or
more having some degree of disability. In the United States references to 1 in 7 of the population, or about 27 million, having a
permanent impairment are common, although the usefulness of
such statistics may be doubted. The President's Commission on
Chronic Illness which produced this figure itself pointed out that
most of the people involved did not require specialized facilities
or services.

The Government national survey of the disabled in Britain was
undertaken partly as a result of the skilful and determined pressure
brought to bear by the Disablement Income Group. DIG was started
in 1965 by two housewives who were themselves newly disabled by
multiple sclerosis, an unpredictable degenerative disease of the

central nervous system which usually affects young adults, which has no known cause or cure, and which brings increasing paralysis in its later stages. Faced in middle life with such a devastating personal situation, Mrs Megan Du Boisson[6] and Mrs Berit Moore discovered that many people with disabilities were even worse off than themselves, since they both had husbands with above-average incomes. They found that a great many people not only had to cope with the problems of disablement itself, but were also living in varying degrees of poverty and deprivation. They started DIG to try to remedy this situation.

Eight years later the Disablement Income Group is a nationwide organization, with forty local branches throughout the country. It has a membership of over 10,000, made up of both the disabled and of interested supporters. The Group has received a great deal of publicity through the press, radio and television, and has the backing of most of the voluntary and professional bodies in the field. It can claim to have played a large part in bringing the needs of the disabled before the public and the Government, and in stimulating various expressions of concern for their problems. There have been several Private Members' Bills presented to Parliament, and the disabled have received frequent mention in debates. The Government has made certain extra social security provisions. And there have been rallies, lobbies, and resolutions at party conferences and many other national gatherings.

The sort of deprivation DIG has been revealing is startling in a society which prides itself on its Welfare State. It is true that in many respects Britain is one of the best countries in the world in which to be disabled, with its network of social security arrangements, the National Health Service, local authority health and social service departments, special education and training facilities, and the array of voluntary organizations. Nevertheless there are huge gaps in both the social security system and the health and welfare services, and we are still a long way from having the kind of comprehensive provision which the disabled really need, and which a country as rich as ours can afford. This applies with particular force to the question of income maintenance.

The Disablement Income Group has highlighted the fact that from the financial point of view there are two distinct classes of people who are disabled—much as there are two nations in old

age, according to Richard Titmuss. Those in the first group have at least a reasonably adequate income drawn from one or more sources. They may have acquired sufficient private resources through high earnings before disablement, through inheritance, or through marriage. They may have received compensation for an accident, or have been insured privately against becoming handicapped. They may in some cases be able to work and earn a good living despite disablement. Finally, and most importantly for purposes of comparison, there are people who have become disabled while in the armed services, or as a result of their paid work, and who therefore receive reasonably scaled state pensions and allowances. A very severely handicapped man in these last two categories, married and with two dependent children, might in 1973 receive up to £40 a week—above the average industrial wage for men—made up of a basic pension plus various allowances. Should he become able to return to work despite his handicap he would still retain his basic weekly pension—up to £11.20 at present rates. If his pension was less than this amount, and his capacity to earn had been diminished by disablement, he would also be paid a loss-of-earnings supplement in compensation.

In contrast to this relatively well-off group are the hundreds of thousands of men and women who may suffer from equally severe or worse handicaps, but who are not fortunate enough to have any of these sources of income. There are several major categories in this neglected group. Firstly, the severely disabled person who has worked but whose disability arises *other* than as a result of his or her paid employment or while he was in the services (for example, as a result of multiple sclerosis, rheumatoid arthritis, or accidents at home), may be entitled only to Invalidity Benefit plus allowances for any dependents. Often this has to be made up by Supplementary Benefit, but at 1973 rates for a married man with two dependent children this means a total income of perhaps £15–£18 a week, plus an allowance for rent. This includes both the long-term addition of 50p a week payable after two years' receipt of benefit and family allowances. The Supplementary Benefits Commission is in addition able to make certain 'exceptional needs' payments to the long-term sick and disabled, both in the form of weekly allowances and of lump sums, but it is known that these extra payments in fact average out at less than 50p a week per person, and in November

1970 were given to only 20 per cent of the 170,000 sick or disabled persons who had been receiving Supplementary Benefit for two years or more.[7] There can be no question of such 'special provision' being remotely adequate in the vast majority of cases.

An early letter from DIG's files, typical of many received through the years, illustrates something of what this situation can mean to a family. In 1967, after thirty years in work, the writer of the letter was unemployed and registered disabled. His income from Sickness Benefit and allowances amounted to £8 13s 6d a week, on which he had to keep himself, his wife and their fourteen-year-old son. The rent alone came to £2 4s 5d. He said : 'We do not have meat in our family now, we cannot afford it.' This family was not in fact even receiving the minimum laid down by the Supplementary Benefits Commission because, like many others, the husband was affected by the 'wage stop' (the regulation which stipulates that no one can receive more in benefits than the average amount per week he was earning when last in employment). The application of this rule to the long-term disabled has been modified, and also the benefits payable to a man in similar circumstances are today higher in real terms. But these improvements have not eliminated the poverty of many individuals and families. 120,000 'Invalidity Pensioners' were still dependent on Supplementary Benefit in November 1970 according to the DHSS Annual Report for that year.

A second important category of neglect involves an estimated 200,000 severely handicapped married women under the age of 65 who are not eligible for any state benefits in respect of their disablement. Women who run their homes and bring up their children are not considered to be 'gainfully employed', and so are not insurable under State schemes. Unless the housewife also happens to be working outside the home when she becomes disabled, or has recently been in paid work for at least three years, she cannot claim Invalidity Benefit. If her husband is working she is not even eligible for Supplementary Benefit, however low his income may be. For assessment purposes she is considered as an extension of her husband, and no one in full-time employment may receive help.

Another letter received by DIG illustrates this second large area of need, and also gives some idea of the kind of strain that lack of financial help can put on families with a disabled member. It is from a man whose wife has been practically helpless for five years following a stroke. He writes :

> In order to pay my way I have to work at least six hours over-time, which means I am away from home eleven hours a day. I have to get up just after 5.0 a.m. to prepare my wife's midday meal and our breakfast and to get her washed and dressed and leave the place tidy. I return home at 6.10 p.m. but only to start work again. Sometimes I feel I'd like to run out and leave it all behind, but the ties are too great. I hope I shall always feel this way.

Faced with this kind of situation some husbands give up work to look after their wives and children, and they all then exist on Supplementary Benefit. Some men, understandably, cannot face such a struggle, so their wives go into hospital (often one for the aged and dying) and the children have to be taken into care. Yet as DIG has pointed out so often, the cost of a hospital bed for the wife, plus the cost of keeping the children in care, would cover several times over what it needs to keep the family together, even if this included payment for nursing and domestic help at home. It is true that a proportion of families would still break up under the other strains that disablement brings. But if adequate help were available there would be at least a better chance of survival.

A third group hard-hit by the present lack of comprehensive provision is that of about 150,000 physically or mentally handicapped men and women who either have never been able to enter employment, or whose contribution record is insufficient to qualify them for insurance benefits. They therefore face a lifetime of subsistence on Supplementary Benefit, with no prospect of ever attaining a standard of living comparable with that of the majority in this country. Usually they are unmarried, and therefore do not enjoy the care and services that married people often receive from their partners and children. People in this category are entitled at 1973 rates to £7.40 a week Supplementary Benefit plus a rent allowance (which amounts to only 65p a week if they are non-householders living with relatives or elsewhere).

Fourthly, at present no special allowances or tax concessions are made to many families which are bringing up a severely handicapped child at home. Fifthly, there are no allowances, except once again the most inadequate Supplementary Benefit additions, for the majority of elderly people who are disabled or sick but who are struggling to manage at home on the basic retirement pension. The constant attendance allowance introduced in November 1971 and extended in October 1972 helps only a minority of the needy in all the five categories described so far.

Lastly, there are the many low wage-earners who have some degree of physical or mental handicap. It is thought that they may account for a considerable proportion of the thousands of families which live at or below the subsistence level laid down by the Supplementary Benefits Commission. The present social security system for the 'civilian' disabled gives no special help to the person whose pay is low because of disability, although the Conservative Government's ill-conceived Family Income Supplement Scheme may do this incidentally in a very small way.

It is also worth mentioning that many of the long-term unemployed receiving Supplementary Benefit are likely to be disabled in some degree, although not actually registered as such. In addition, amongst those who *are* officially registered with the Department of Employment and Productivity as disabled but capable of full-time work, the unemployment figure is 14 per cent (1972 figure). Even this does not show the true rate of unemployment amongst the disabled, because many who would be capable of some work are not included on the Department's register if they are considered unable to hold down a full-time job.

It is not possible to go into the question of employment in any detail here, but clearly it is relevant to the financial situation of the disabled. One of the strongest desires of most disabled people is to be able to do an ordinary job of work. Unfortunately, in a great many cases the opportunities for them to do so are limited by their handicaps, and also by deficiencies in facilities for rehabilitation, training and retraining, by inadequate help from Disablement Resettlement Officers, and by prejudice amongst employers and employees. For the most severely disabled there is a lack of suitable home-work schemes. Where work of any kind *is* obtained, all too often it is menial and/or underpaid.

The sort of impact that the lack of any proper financial provision for disablement has in the community was shown in some detail by Professor Townsend's survey. He says :

> Altogether 60 per cent of the households surveyed had a total income of less than £10 a week, and another 36 per cent less than £20. (A third of the households, it should be remembered, contained three or more persons.) Three quarters had less than £50 savings. Nearly half depended partly or wholly on National Assistance and about 5 per cent might have qualified for supplementary assistance had they applied for it. There is no doubt that a disproportionately large number of the disabled live in poverty or on its margins.[8]

Similarly, the 1967 Tower Hamlets Survey[9] found that only 17 disabled people out of 201 interviewed had an income of more than £10 a week.[10]

Low as these income figures were by any standards in this country, they do not by themselves tell the whole story. It must be appreciated that disability usually involves various extra expenses for the individual and his or her family. There may be additional wear and tear on clothes and shoes, special equipment and accessories may be desirable, and extra heating is often necessary for those whose mobility is restricted. When the disabled person has to spend many hours alone a telephone can become an essential. Going out, whether to work or for social reasons, may be particularly expensive, because public transport is often difficult or impossible to use. For the man who would normally do much of his home maintenance himself, disability will probably mean employing workmen instead. The housewife may find her ability to run the home and bring up her children greatly reduced or lost altogether, and she therefore has to pay something for home-help. Most local authorities only supply this free where income is around Supplementary Benefit level, and in any case the home-help service, like many others which local authorities provide, is usually quite inadequate to meet the demands placed on it. Again, for some people it is necessary to employ assistance with nursing or daily care, and here the local authority services are even more unlikely to be of use.

All these extra expenses caused by disablement may, of course, be a burden to those who are in work or whose relatives are maintaining them, as well as to those receiving social security. As we have seen, the extra State help given with such special expenses, even to those on Supplementary Benefit, is wholly inadequate, and in any case involves degrading forms of application. The same comments apply with equal force to most sources of financial help from voluntary societies.

The implications of the lack of adequate financial provision for many of the disabled, and the extra expenditure they may incur, can be seen clearly in the area of housing. Peter Townsend and Sally Sainsbury[11] found that 20 per cent of their sample were living in houses which were deficient in three or more basic facilities, such as an indoor lavatory, a hot-water supply, or a bath. In Tower Hamlets[12] 38 per cent of the sample had no inside lavatory, and 45 per cent no bath. Both surveys showed that stairs were also a major difficulty. In the Townsend study 74 per cent had to use flights of stairs either inside or outside their accommodation, while 33 per cent had to negotiate stairs inside *and* outside. In Tower Hamlets almost 40 per cent had to use a flight of stairs to reach their homes, and in many cases more than one. A lot of the most inadequate housing in both surveys was privately rented, and the tenants had sometimes been on local authority waiting lists for many years. The Government national survey estimated that 15,000 severely handicapped people needed rehousing, and 75,000 required structural alterations to their accommodation : it confirmed that the lack of basic facilities occurs mainly in private rented accommodation. Only one-fifth of householders in Townsend's sample were buying their own houses, as compared with two-fifths of the general population. Apart from lack of the necessary income, mortgages are in any case difficult or impossible to come by for people who are not medically fit at the time of application.

Besides the basic deficiencies of a good proportion of the houses in which the disabled live, there are indications of many failures on the part of local authorities to carry out minor adaptations and provide aids which are clearly needed. Townsend quotes high figures for disabled occupants who could not open or shut windows, use the gas or electricity meter, turn taps, use a sink, or reach cupboards.

Where special aids *had* been provided they were usually simple ones which made life much easier. The beneficial psychological effect of retaining one's independence in daily living activities, and in entering and leaving one's home, scarcely needs pointing out, and its importance for long-term relationships within the family must be equally plain. Townsend calls for local authorities to give the disabled greater priority on housing lists. He also proposes special local authority work forces to execute a carefully planned blitz of adaptations on suitable dwellings when an occupant becomes disabled.

The slowly emerging picture of widespread poverty and hardship amongst the disabled, together with the pressure for reform brought to bear by the Disablement Income Group and other organizations and individuals, drew from the Wilson government many statements that they were aware of and sympathetic to the problems of the long-term sick and disabled. As a sign of their concern they helped Alfred Morris's Chronically Sick and Disabled Persons Bill to become law just before the 1970 general election. The main feature of this legislation was an attempt to compel local authorities to expand their social services for the disabled living at home, and there were various other miscellaneous provisions. It is to be hoped that the Act will in particular eventually prod local authorities into making more satisfactory provision for home care, but the Government has not pressed for its full implementation, and it has been easy for many councils to evade their apparent obligations—if only by imposing stringent means tests. The Act has never been quite the charter for the future of the disabled that has been claimed. And the danger is that, with so much publicity giving the impression that a great deal more is now being done, it may tend to obscure the central question of income maintenance.

The Labour Government also had several financial proposals for the disabled in the pipeline when the election was held. The chief one was for a new earnings-related sickness benefit to become payable, following the six months short-term sickness benefit, to men and women who were covered under the National Insurance Scheme when they became permanently disabled and had to stop work. The Disablement Income Group resisted the Labour Government's attempts to describe this 'premature retirement' pension as an invalidity pension, because it had no element of scaling for the degree of handicap and made no attempt to compensate for the extra expenses resulting from disablement. The scheme would have created new anomalies between those disabled early and late in life, and between those with more or less severe handicaps. It also did nothing for people who had never been able to work. In the event this proposal was lost when Labour failed to be re-elected.

Rather more satisfactory was the other main Labour Government proposal, which was improved on and enacted by the Conservatives as soon as they took office. From November 1971 a tax-free, non-means-tested, non-contributory constant attendance allowance has been paid to those who need frequent day and night care. Children, the elderly, and the mentally handicapped are included. Originally, an estimated 50,000 people were expected to benefit by £4.80 a week. But by March 1972, 75,000 awards had already been made. (This take-up rate is in marked contrast to the 50 per cent rate for the Conservative Government's *means-tested* Family Income Supplement, which extends a small supplementary benefit to the lowest paid workers with children.) In October 1972 the full attendance allowance was increased to £5.40, and a new reduced rate of £3.60 became payable to people needing *either* day or night attendance. Government estimates were that eventually about 250,000 would qualify at the reduced rate.

This constant attendance allowance undoubtedly represents a significant advance for the severely disabled of this country, establishing as it does several important new principles from which a more equitable system could grow. But three points must be made about the allowance. Firstly, many people in need will not qualify for it—those who struggle on and manage to look after themselves, for instance. Secondly, the comparable allowances for the war and industrially disabled can amount to as much as £13 a week. And thirdly, it must be evident that not even these allowances would cover the cost of frequent nursing help to keep a very severely handicapped person at home.

Apart from the attendance allowance, which applied only to the most heavily disabled, nothing was proposed by the 1964–70 Labour Government for the thousands of housewives who receive no help at all, or for virtually all the other groups which have been mentioned as needing comprehensive state cover in adversity. But what was most disturbing about Labour's policies was their revelation of a fundamental failure to consider the question at the level required. Basically they appeared to be content with the system much as it was.[13] When Richard Crossman was Minister of Health and Social Security he wrote to the Disablement Income Group saying that he regarded Supplementary Benefit, on which so many disabled people are reliant, as 'a fair and sensible means of helping a lot of people'. Yet from so many angles means-tested Supplementary Benefit is a most inappropriate form of assistance for 'the poor' and particularly for those who have special long-term needs arising from disablement. This is recognized where the war and industrially disabled are concerned, and there seems no reason why the 'civilian' disabled should be treated differently.

When the Conservatives were in opposition they made helpful noises about the need for a proper disability pension, and to their credit they were quick to implement and extend the new attendance allowance. But judging from their Family Income Supplement scheme, they are in practice even more content than Labour with large-scale recourse to means-tested subsistence allowances. The general Tory approach to welfare benefits and services does not augur well for the disabled and other handicapped minorities, and it seems unlikely that the party of selectivity and the 'lame duck' philosophy will ever be able to tackle the question in the manner required. Their pensions Act, due to come into operation in 1975, makes no mention of disability.[14] The latest government proposal for a form of 'negative income tax' leaves out 10 per cent of the population, including it seems most of the non-employed disabled, and the Supplementary Benefits system will remain.

What the Conservative Government has actually done, in addition to legislating for the attendance allowance, is to introduce certain extra payments for people receiving Sickness Benefit after six months of incapacity. From September 1971 a small 'Invalidity Pension' of up to £1 a week (depending on the age at which incapacity starts) has been paid, plus extra children's allowances. Wives of invalidity pensioners are also allowed to earn up to £9.50 —instead of £3.10—without loss of benefit.

This scheme is not so different from the Labour proposals and it is open to the same basic objections. Although it may be seen as a move towards giving the National Insurance pensioner parity with the industrially disabled, it introduces new anomalies by leaving out both the disabled housewife and those handicapped so early in life that they have never been able to make sufficient contributions to qualify for benefit. Apparently it is intended in 1975 to reduce the qualifying contribution period from a minimum of three years to that of one, but of course this will still exclude large numbers of people. There is no element of scaling for degree of disablement; and retention of the traditional 'all or nothing' approach means that invalidity pensioners themselves are still harshly discouraged from undertaking part-time work although for some this would be both feasible and highly desirable. Incidentally, one of the ironies of this new-style increase was that about half the 400,000 beneficiaries lost some or all of their entitlement to Supplementary Benefit and ended up no better off.

It is understandable that for historical and other reasons the contributory principle is felt to be important. But an overriding principle of fairness demands that some means be found of bringing everyone within a truly comprehensive scheme. The Disablement Income Group contends that if a national insurance scheme is to be truly national—like the National Health Service—it should offer adequate cover against disablement to everyone. So housewives should be brought into the scheme either on their husband's contributions or on their own. People who have been too handicapped to work through disablement from childhood should be franked into the scheme at the age of sixteen, with special allowances being payable to their parents before this age. The basic pension should be paid even to those who can earn or who have private resources, but it should be taxable so that those in least need receive least benefit. People who are unable to work at all should receive the full pension, with a reduced rate being payable to those assessed as able to work despite substantial disablement. All the appreciably handicapped ought also to get a special tax-free allowance, solely to meet their unavoidable extra living expenses.

It is important that a comprehensive new scheme should recognize clearly, with appropriate rates of benefit, the difference between the category of short-term sickness, on the one hand, and that of permanent disablement with its special needs, on the other. At the

moment, someone in bed for a week with flu may receive virtually
the same insurance benefit as someone facing a life-time of total
paralysis, or dying slowly of cancer. It is obvious that Sickness
Benefit and other allowances are scaled, even with earnings-related
supplements, simply to tide people over limited periods off work,
not for years of disablement. In the short term, most people can
dig into savings or cut down on luxuries to get by. A longer period
off work may mean a few debts or an overdraft at the bank, but
these can be put right when things get back to normal. Permanent reliance on state benefits, perhaps with a growing family
to cater for, and certainly with extra expenses arising out of the
disablement, is a very different matter. It requires very different
provision.

Clearly, no matter how it is arranged, the first priority is to get
much more money quickly to many seriously disadvantaged individuals and families. This would not only relieve intolerable strain
immediately, but would eventually have various desirable social
consequences—fewer children growing up in poverty, for example,
and some families being saved from breaking up. The mere fact
that the equation 'disability equals poverty' would occur less often
would in itself help the disabled to participate more in society. Very
low economic status adds extra barriers to those associated with
disablement and physical dependency in our society.

But even in the unlikely event of Supplementary Benefit rates
being raised to an adequate level for the disabled, special disability
allowances becoming payable to those in work, to disabled housewives, and to families with handicapped children, the situation
would still not be satisfactory. It is not simply a question of having
enough money. The way in which the money is made available is
extremely important. If disability could become one of the eventual-
ities against which every member of every family was adequately
insured under the National Insurance Scheme, this would help to
make the fact of disablement, and its special needs, a reality to the
whole population as something that can happen to us all. It would
also help to create a climate in which people who are at any given
time disabled are thought of as 'people like us' rather than as 'them'
—a quite separate and stigmatized category 'looked after by the
Assistance Board and the charities'. To see the importance of this
point it is necessary to abandon the usual vision of a large group of

fit, normal people (us) regarding a small group of poor unfortunates (them). Instead it has to be recognized that everyone is at least potentially a member of the second group, and that the standards thought right for the majority should govern the kind of provision to be made for the whole community without exception. Basing a campaign for a decent state pension for the disabled mainly on the premise that everyone ought to be adequately insured against the chance of becoming handicapped or having a handicapped child, should be more successful and more constructive socially than attempts to stimulate generosity for a pitied minority.

A comprehensive social security system must be the first priority on any scale of the needs of the disabled. But as I have said it would be wrong to give the impression that all their problems would be solved if adequate finance was by some miracle provided overnight. There are many other difficulties in the lives of the disabled— although in fact they are often closely related to the economic problem. There is the unsuitability of arrangements for the severely impaired, thousands of whom languish in large residential institutions. Tragically, Sir Keith Joseph was at the 1972 Conservative Party Conference boasting of his record in building many more such institutions than Labour, when what is urgently needed is suitable ordinary housing with background care provided, as in the Fokus schemes in Sweden. I have already touched on the inadequacy or non-existence of many local authority services which may make institutionalization necessary in the first place : this situation is not going to be transformed just by the passing of the Alf Morris Act. I have also indicated that the need for employment with dignity is a particularly vital question where the disabled are concerned. Then there are the various anomalies in state help with personal transport, and the need to eliminate architectural barriers such as flights of steps to public libraries and lavatories.

Grave deficiencies exist in educational provision for handicapped children and young adults. Medical and social rehabilitation facilities for certain groups such as housewives, the elderly, the mentally handicapped, and the very severely disabled, come in for increasing criticism. Despite progress in recent years, much more could usefully be done in the field of sport and recreation, both by enabling the disabled to participate as far as they can and by ensuring that audience and spectator arrangements are suitable.

I would suggest also that, despite the excellent rescue work some of them undertake, a large proportion of the voluntary societies concerned with the disabled are ripe for reform, amalgamation or abolition. It seems to me that many of their problems stem from the poverty of the disabled and the consequent necessity for raising large sums from the public and other sources. Such legalized begging, with its often degrading stimulation of feelings of pity and guilt, breeds a sense of superiority in the fund-raisers and donors, and produces subservience and a sense of stigma in the recipients. The constant emphasis on the need for money corrupts and trivializes relations between the disabled and the public. There is also unfairness in the present competition for a limited amount of charitable resources. Some causes have a natural appeal—cats and dogs and young children, for example—but the aged and mentally handicapped do not evoke the same kind of response, although their relative needs may be greater.

Perhaps in the long term the most important drawback of the present system is that the need to raise so much money helps to ensure that many voluntary societies do not tackle problems at their roots. The financial advantages of registered charity status are considerable, but the Charity Commissioners insist that no charity may campaign for political change. The result is to help emasculate a number of organizations which ought to be active politically if they are to fulfil their aims properly.

Apart from the areas discussed above where reform is needed, there remain the personal difficulties which may accompany disablement, such as pain, fatigue, depression, loneliness and frustration. Perhaps money cannot directly relieve problems like these, although the assignment of bigger Government funds for medical research would help in the long term, but it seems to me that the right kind of arrangements for income maintenance are as important as good medical services in providing an encouraging basis for the many positive developments which can also result from disablement. Even very severe disability need not turn out to be the fate worse than death that most people assume it to be. Many of the physically handicapped find that in time their physical and medical problems cease to be a constant preoccupation, and become more of a background nuisance. They turn their attention to the question of participation in ordinary life, refusing to think of themselves as totally 'sick', but rather as disabled in some respects and not in others. In education, work, and family and social life, attempts are made to break down the barriers and prejudices between themselves and the rest of society. This is not a matter of denying their need for special compensatory help, but of a feeling that such assistance ought not to diminish anyone's right to be treated as a full member of the community.

This implicit challenge to some of the prevailing values of society seems to me a healthier response to the personal experience of disability than the acceptance of a dependent and unequal position as a helpless invalid. But there are powerful social and psychological pressures on the disabled person to give in and adopt the largely passive role which is traditionally expected of him. For this reason alone it is important that our social security system and social services should be designed to eliminate stigmatizing poverty and to encourage every impulse towards rehabilitation and participation in society.

Finally, the present situation of many of the physically disabled in this country cannot be considered without reference to that of other groups which are handicapped in one way or another—by old age, by mental breakdown or impairment, by all the conditions covered in this book. It is, I believe, time for the Disablement Income Group to get together with bodies such as Shelter, Age Concern and the Child Poverty Action Group, to try to work out a common strategy for change. The continued existence of seriously disadvantaged minorities in our relatively rich society poses far-reaching questions about that society's values and priorities, and particularly about whether the present distribution of resources is the best that can or ought to be achieved. The Labour Party in office effectively abandoned any idea of redistribution in favour of the poor, while the Conservatives have shown themselves to be set on redistribution in favour of the rich. It is evident, however, that the plight of the various under-privileged minorities will not be remedied except by a major shift of available resources in their favour and an associated transformation of our approach towards equality and social justice.

It is tempting to imagine that all the problems of poverty will sort themselves out if our standard of living continues to rise. But although the situation of the disabled and other similarly placed groups may be improving slowly in *absolute* terms, their *relative* share of the country's resources is if anything decreasing, and therefore they remain in poverty compared with the majority—and even more so compared with the affluent minority. This failure of the idea of automatic progress towards the elimination of poverty, on both a national and an international level, has become clear in recent years. It is equally clear that the pursuit of unlimited economic growth may be said to be leading to disaster. In searching for the principles and means by which the disabled may be helped to share fully in our national life, we are confronting one aspect of what is perhaps the central moral and political challenge of our time.

[I am grateful to Phyllis Willmott for her comments on an early version of this essay. She is not of course responsible for any remaining factual errors or for the opinions expressed. P.H.]

NOTES

1 Peter Townsend, *The Disabled in Society* (Greater London Association for the Disabled, 1967). Lecture based on a survey of 211 men and women registered as physically handicapped with local authorities in London, Essex and Middlesex. A detailed report of the survey, by Sally Sainsbury, was published by the GLAD in December 1970.

2 S. Goldsmith, *Designing for the Disabled* (RIBA, 1967), p. 54.

3 Townsend, *op. cit.*, p. 1.

4 Amelia I. Harris, *Handicapped and Impaired in Great Britain* (HMSO, 1971), vol. i. Judith R. Buckle, *Work and Housing of Impaired Persons in Great Britain* (HMSO, 1971), vol. ii.

5 Although the survey provides much useful information, some vital questions were not covered, and the main section on income is still not published.

6 Until her death in a road accident in 1969, Mrs Du Boisson's legendary charm and determination were a major factor in the Disablement Income Group's rapid growth.

7 DHSS figure quoted in *Creating a National Disability Income* (DIG Occasional Paper 12, 1972).

8 Townsend, *op. cit.*, pp. 18–19.

9 Frank W. Skinner (ed.), *Physical Disability and Community Care* (Bedford Square Press, NCSS, 1969). Survey of 201 people registered with the Borough of Tower Hamlets as physically handicapped.

10 It should be noted that two-fifths of the Townsend sample, and half of that in Tower Hamlets, were aged 65 or over. The few available income figures from the 1968–9 Government survey, with again nearly half those interviewed being elderly, confirm the picture of widespread hardship.

11 Townsend, *op. cit.*, pp. 9–11.

12 Skinner, *op. cit.*

13 Encouragingly, their 1972 policy Green Paper seems to accept the principle of a disability benefit payable as a right and based on need rather than on contribution record. It remains to be seen, however, what happens to the proposal as it is spelled out in more detail.

14 Unhappily, DIG's proposals involve the acceptance of earnings-related disability pensions, which in my view would mean the further creation and perpetuation of inequalities and anomalies. Purely in cash terms, too, earnings-related benefits would be ineffective; their value would tend to be small because of the low earnings associated with disablement, and they would in any case be paid only to a small minority of the disabled.

PAUL WIDLAKE

Adolescence and Educational Failure

The English educational system does not produce an exact equivalent to the American 'drop-out'. A Schools Council report on
socially disadvantaged children[1] suggests, however, that a substantial
number 'contract-out' of a system which to them has become remote
and, to a greater or lesser extent, alien. These pupils observe the
educational scene in something like the same spirit in which English
punters play the Australian football pools : the game is familiar,
they await the final whistle with ill-concealed impatience, but it is
all slightly unreal, impersonal—Antipodean. It is just not their
scene, and they are either bored and apathetic or resentful and
aggressive. With the raising of the school-leaving age, many more
will join the considerable numbers who express their disdain for the
vastly expensive state educational system by staying away from
school altogether. All this is distressing to the providers of universal
education but, surely, not surprising.

There are at least two grounds upon which a cynical view of
public educational provision may be based. In the first place, it is
a matter of common observation that nearly all those parents who
can afford to buy their children out of the State system, do so, and
effectively signal to everyone else the message that there is another
and better system. It is by no means clear that the growth of so-
called comprehensive schools will do anything much to diminish
this polarization. On the contrary, it is likely that Education will
follow the National Health and Employment services, used by the
middle classes only as a last resort and by the upper classes not at
all. The antagonism felt by the 'contracting-out' pupils towards
State schools is, in one sense, merely a reflection of the disdain
implicit in the reluctance of society as a whole to use the public

services. 'Schools for other people's children' : a notorious politician was reputed to have dismissed an educational delegation with these contemptuous words. The worst of it is, many teachers have accepted this explanation of their work. 'We only get the dregs here,' explained the headteacher of a brand-new educational palace in a mint-fresh Council estate, apologizing in advance for his pupils' poor attainment. The movement to establish 'parity of esteem' for the secondary modern schools in the years immediately following the Second World War was undermined and eventually destroyed by the public's inability to consider the possibilities of a non-examinable curriculum, but also by the lack of conviction with which the teaching profession itself propounded the possibilities. All these hesitations, doubts, heart-burnings have been clearly expressed in the local and national debates on 'going comprehensive', especially since Circular 10/65. Many pupils are fully aware of the issues involved and their own states of restlessness or withdrawal reflect the prevailing English educational pandemonium.

We shall be less surprised to find a number of pupils at odds with the educational system if we observe, secondly, that universal education is a recent innovation, a noble ideal which has never as yet been fully realized anywhere in the world. Some, like R. S. Peters, might argue that education, an initiation into worthwhile activities, by definition implies an elite, and that the citadel of learning can shelter only those who possess (or acquire) the ability to succeed in pre-determined initiation rites. Thus 'universal education' is impossible, unless we enlarge the definition of 'education' to cover a much wider spectrum of activities than is usually subsumed under that head in this country. With the growth of courses designed to meet the requirements of the new school leavers, often under the umbrella of CSE Mode III examinations which encourage personal achievement, new perspectives in this controversy may appear, but there are fundamental and difficult questions to be posed and (in the English tradition) determined empirically.

Consider the implications of universal education in terms of the population involved. Some form of selection or modification of entry has almost always operated—even at Summerhill, A. S. Neill has always retained the right to determine entry, and also the power of expulsion. This safety valve is not available to the head of a non-selective secondary school : a pupil who commits an outrage such

as an act of arson can be excluded, but for the most part the doors
are open to all comers within the age range. The highways and byways are surveyed and the morally halt and the emotionally blind
are not merely invited to the feast, they are compelled to attend,
by court order if necessary. A few of the most obviously handicapped
pupils are sent to special schools but the vast majority of educationally sub-normal (ESN) and a considerable proportion of the physically handicapped, receive their education within the ordinary
system. Special provision for emotionally disturbed children is sparse,
and often they too must be catered for in the non-selective secondary
school. All these constitute, as it were, the normal 'at risk' population
of universal education, even when the system is on-going and func-
tioning well. Taking England and Wales as a whole, and considering the hazardous nature of the enterprise, things do go rather well
in both the ordinary and the special school systems. But it can sur-
prise no one, surely, that significant numbers of boys and girls have
difficulty in threading their way through this educational maze.

The Disenchanted

Then there are those who suffer from a form of ideological dis-
location. Some are in the process of discovering the realities of
capitalist society and, urged on by a gaggle of irresponsible social
workers, educational journalists in hot pursuit of a best seller and
television producers running short on newszak, put considerable
energy into organizing petitions against school uniforms and similar
intolerable restrictions on their liberty. Ample media coverage en-
sures that this side of pupil discontent attracts attention and comment out of all proportion to its importance. School uniforms *will*
be abolished, Councils *will* be formed in all secondary schools but,
their objectives achieved, the revolutionaries will find the chore of
consultation a heavy weight: at Countesthorpe, in Leicestershire,
where these ideas have been fully developed, pupils no longer bother
to turn up to council meetings because they observed that a few
fluent teachers dominated the proceedings and only the most vocal
students feel adequate to contribute. Some schools cling to savagely
authoritarian regimes, and opposition here (as in South Africa)
requires considerable courage; but the climate of opinion is in

favour of change and before long the outward trappings of pupil participation will become standard fittings in all up-to-date schools. It can be predicted with some confidence that none of this will have much effect on the pupils' attitudes to education. The boy quoted at the beginning of the Newsom Report[2] was unequivocal in his belief that whatever improvements were effected to the fabric, 'it would still be a bloody school'. The same reasoning applies to uniforms, pupil representation and the other well-publicized 'revolutionary' demands : they are peripheral to the world of those who have contracted-out, most of whom have never had a school uniform to react against.

Much more serious is the plight of the pupil who is bright enough to be an examination aspirant but can hope to pass only by investing enormous physical and mental resources. Such pupils tend to develop unrealistic expectations about, for example, the possible effects of examination successes on their daily lives. The existence of many graduate Asian bus drivers and conductors has not, apparently, diminished the faith that Asians have in the acquisition of English qualifications. Some West Indians push on painfully over 'O' level and CSE hurdles, only to find that employers select applicants for jobs on criteria quite other than examination successes.

Others are romantically at odds with society :

Although I remember many good times from my schooldays, I feel that the daily monotony and fear and hatred of some subjects and teachers, may have helped the lighter moments to have lingered in my memory. School was never designed to be a 'playground of happiness' though, was it? 'A passage of hopefulness' might be a more acceptable definition.

Corridors of time

A very long passage, a corridor with hundreds of rooms, each with its own labelled door, on either side. It takes a child ten or more years to reach the other end. During this corridor of time the pupil must enter every door in its room, a degree of freely offered knowledge will be acquired. School is a main factor in the processing of the human mind. The simple, happy, innocent infant is passed through school and comes out, brain bursting with complexities, less innocent and almost certainly less happy. He or she has emerged, the finished product. To be hopefully regarded as a useful member of Society. A Society that requires both success and failure to fit into place. The navvy and the prospective architect both have to answer to their questions. Is he strong, willing, obedient? Is he qualified, ambitious, dedicated? Remember the raw material, well, the raw material is completely forgotten. The very core eaten away.

David Patchett[3] wrote those words about the educational experiences which had caused him, in his late teens, to drop out of society: he had ceased even to attend to his personal hygiene. As he saw it :

Education, and its use in the earning of money, had crammed my swirling head with useless information, had stretched out a tedious waste of living time over my youth and finally, had begun a prolonged attack on my individuality and sanity. I controlled myself and began the inquiry; back to the uncarved block. Why have I been born? No conclusive answer. Well then, as I have been what shall I do while I'm here? The reply seemed reasonable. Search for happiness in goodness, beginning with the stamping out of misery in badness. So I began stomping around with Jesus, Buddha, Socrates, and later Bob Dylan, struggling in their appointed capacity as guiding lights. Inevitably I became a nomad; untidy in appearance and without material wealth, these changes were hints of improvement. But, all was not well. Although I felt I carried a message I was without audience. No one joined me and I soon observed that I was discounted by my brothers as a half-crazed layabout. For the thousandth time in my twenty years a question came to burn within, it fired. 'Is it them, or me?'[4]

The Socially Disadvantaged

Pupils who are disenchanted with school life and society in general can be found in all schools and in all districts, but everyone recognizes the special problems of the inner-city schools. Certain neighbourhoods are known in every city for a combination of delapidated housing, crime and vice. There is a good deal of quite genuine poverty and much actual want, brought about by domestic mismanagement or improvidence. Ethnic-based prejudice is always present, though usually just below the surface of daily affairs, which are dominated by getting and spending to an extent not easily grasped by middle-class observers. Whatever forces threaten the stability of society at large will appear like volcanic eruptions at these weak spots.

The type of pupil to be found in these areas has been well described by a conference of head teachers (seventeen headmasters and fifteen headmistresses) in two Reports issued by the Department of Education and Science (No. 17, 1964; No. 18, 1965). All the heads taking part were known to have had some success in difficult social or physical or occupational environments, and they were invited to come together and discuss their experiences. They began by identifying two elements, the handicaps arising in the home environment and those arising at school. Considerable numbers of pupils came from broken homes, or were illegitimate, or had parents in prison. Others had endured the shock of eviction. Sheer lack of parental interest was another factor making for early retardation from which most of the children never recovered. In many homes there were no books, seldom any story telling, and the child received little help in developing his powers of communication. Working mothers were often not accessible to their children at the times of day when they needed them most and were too tired to show interest at other times. Poor health and poor school attendance often arose from lack of parental concern. The children were not clean, and minor illnesses and physical defects, e.g. slight deafness, went unremarked and untreated. Beset by so many handicaps, the children from such homes lost ground all through the infant and junior school. By the time they reached secondary school they had sunk firmly to the bottom twenty per cent, whatever their latent potential. They constituted primarily a social rather than an educational problem, and teachers were not equipped to meet it.

But there was also a tendency for school life to accentuate these difficulties. School society over-valued the intellect and under-valued qualities of personality. A premium was placed on verbal reasoning ability and the capacity to learn by memorization; success was measured by academic criteria and early failure in acquiring the skills of literacy, numeracy and the capacity to grasp ideas often led to a feeling of rejection among the children afflicted. The growing stress on GCE as the touchstone of success in comprehensive and modern schools set the rejected even more sharply apart.

In these schools, social considerations are frequently the major concern of the staff. The head teacher may spend much of his time interviewing parents about free clothing, free dinners and free bus passes. The pupils' families are larger than the national average and characterized by a higher than average rate of disruption. The children are sometimes unkempt and often (but by no means always) emotionally deprived. The discipline in the home is likely to be unstable, veering from excessive punishment to easy-going indifference. The children show an imbalance in intelligence test scores, frequently showing better results on non-verbal than on verbal scales. Their attention span may be very brief and, in early learning situations, they may reveal a lack of auditory discrimination because of the lack of opportunity for quiet listening in the home. They may value physical prowess more highly than intellectual attainment; more likely, they will show a marked lack of curiosity, an unwillingness to explore new situations.

To take one example of a learning disability, the language used by these pupils frequently reveals auditory distortion. A collection of mispronounced words was made by Miss Q. R. A. Daniels during her ten years of teaching reading at Brighton Remedial Centre. As well as the well-known confusions in the use of 'f', 'v' and 'th', there was 'v' said as 'b', 'st' said as 'sc'; 'am' was spoken as 'and', the word 'belt' said as 'bowt' and also as 'balt' ('a' as in 'sad'). Questions arising in conversations, in reading games and in the reading of books brought the following :

Q. What is a sow?

A. You sell things. . . . A cell in a prison. . . . It's on a yacht. When you have something in your mouth and it's not sweet. Milk is sow. ('sour')

Q. What is a dairy?

A. If someone runs across the road. ('daring' confused with 'dairy')

Q. What is a wharf?

A. An animal. A thing with a long nose. Like a dog. ('wolf')

Q. What is the word Paul?

A. Where you can swim. ('pool')

Q. What is dine?

A. When you darn your stockings.

Q. What is soil?

A. What comes from wood. ('sawdust')

Q. What is a bough?   A. Oh, that's something like a
                                bell.
Q. What is stout?   A. It is on a teapot.

A remark overheard as some children were leaving the centre
was : 'We've got to be quick, or we'll miss the jungle sale.' There
was 'elethant' for 'elephant' and 'thirgitting' for the word 'forgetting'.

Even in the worst parts of the worst slums, the majority of people
strive to maintain a standard of human decency. However, it may
be as well to point out, by introducing a few case histories, that
there is always a number of 'pathological families', and children
from these homes may dominate a class or school. The following
notes were collected by an experienced female interviewer and are
part of a random sample of twenty-five mothers, seen in their own
homes.[5]

1. The first house I visited appeared to be empty and due for
demolition. I looked all round it and was just leaving when a
filthy woman appeared and asked if she could help me. I told
her what I was doing and she asked me inside and said 'you'll
'ave to excuse the place'. I soon saw why! The kitchen was
almost ankle deep in rubbish and when I went into the living
room I was surprised to see that the floor was just earth.* A man
was sitting in an armchair with his feet on the mantelpiece but
stood up when I went in and offered me a cigarette. The room
was indescribably filthy with the wallpaper peeling off revealing
large holes in the wall, and the ceiling was coming down in one
corner. The furniture was greasy with dirt and there was a large
dog chewing a bone on the settee. There was a filthy baby
toddling about who obviously hadn't been washed for several
days. I started the interview and found that every question I
asked was answered by the father after the mother had looked
at him helplessly. I reminded them that it was the mother's
opinion I wanted but she still kept referring to the father. When
I asked what kind of books the child liked, the father said she
liked poetry and that he read a lot of poetry to her. This surprised me but I was even more surprised when I asked the

* During the interview I noticed a pattern in the corner of the 'earth-
floor' and realized that there was a carpet but it was so filthy that it just
looked like earth.

E

father's occupation. He said he had a degree in engineering and had been an experimental engineer until he had a serious accident. He showed me a large scar on his forehead and said he had a silver plate in his head and also a plastic jugular vein. It may all have been lies but he was certainly a more intelligent person than his wife. One can only assume that he married her after his accident.

2. When I went to this house there was a rather fat, balding man of about forty with dyed ginger hair digging in the garden. I asked whether the child's mother was at home and he sent me to the house. The door was opened by a girl of about 20 who said she was the child's mother. As the child was 10 I looked rather puzzled and she said his own mother had died and she was his stepmother. She didn't really know very much about his school life and called his father in to talk to me. The child had run away several times and slept in derelict buildings and the police had brought him back. The father said 'I can't understand him; he was all right when his mother was alive.' He then went off into a bitter tirade about the 'Children's Department' and said he was sick of going because he always had to see somebody different and start all over again. He said the child had stayed out for several nights the week before and at one a.m. he and his wife had gone 'up the entry' to look for him. He caught sight of the child and ran after him and told me that when he came back his wife had been assaulted by two coloured men. He said 'I won't tell you what I said to them but I told them . . .' He then uttered a mouthful of obscene language which he had watered down for my benefit so heaven knows what he really said. He then said 'so the next time the bastard runs away he can stop 'cos I ain't gonna look for him.' We were interrupted at this point by the electricity man coming to cut off the supply for non-payment of the bill. I think there were two or three children of this second marriage.

3. The door was opened by the mother of the child I was interested in. She was fairly young, probably mid-thirties, immensely fat and had a huge black eye. She said I was lucky to have caught her because she was moving that night. She showed me into her room which had a large double bed in it and numerous small children of assorted colours from black through brown to white. She said she was separated from her husband.

The room was dirty with crusts of old bread on the floor and in the fireplace. She said I must excuse the mess but it wasn't worth cleaning it as she was moving. We started the interview and with a great sense of pride she told me her son had been 'in care'. She seemed to be very proud of this as if it were a very desirable place to be. He had been taken 'in care' because he played truant from school and stayed out all night sleeping in empty houses. She was 'sick of sitting in the police station'. However, he had been much better since he had been 'in care' and had only run away twice since Easter (2–3 months before) when he came home. He had run away the week before the interview on Derby Day and the police had found him in Derby. ('He had wanted to see the racing, you see.') She said he was all right if he got to school without seeing an older boy who encouraged him to play truant. I asked whether there were any books in the house for the child to read and she said, 'Oh, yes, we have one somewhere.' She then rummaged in a paper carrier bag and produced a paperback copy of the New Testament and said 'They gave him this "in care".' During the interview various Indian women kept gliding in and out and obviously the house was let off into many separate rooms. When she showed me to the door my curiosity got the better of me and I asked her how she got her black eye. 'Oh that, I had a punch-up with the landlord—that's why I'm moving tonight.'

Cumulative Deficit

The pupils who contract-out become more noticeable at adolescence, but they do not spring forth with a mighty war-shout and in complete armour, like Pallas Athene from the head of Zeus. They have been in much the same relationship to their academic work throughout their school lives. It is not that they change utterly, but that the deficit in academic achievement is cumulative, and early adolescence a critical point on the development scale. 'We need to remember that socially handicapped adolescents have already been socially handicapped children.'[6]

Many recent publications have hammered home this point. The latest report, by the National Bureau for Co-operation in Child Care, on 17,000 children born during a week in March 1958 has documented the class basis of disadvantage in massive detail. Children from unskilled homes are disadvantaged from birth; their disadvantages increase if they belong to large families and if they are badly housed. 'The chances of an unskilled manual worker's child (Social Class V) being a poor reader are six times greater than those of a professional worker's child (Social Class I). If the criterion of poor reading is made more stringent, the disparity is much larger; thus, the chances of a Social Class V child being a non-reader are fifteen times greater than those of a Social Class I child', the study reports.

This pattern persists. It was estimated that proportionately no less than forty-five times as many Social Class V children would have benefited from attending special schools as Social Class I children.

At the age of seven the average reading attainment of the middle-class child is already two years higher than that of the working-class child. That of the middle-class child in a small, secure family with decent living conditions is four years ahead of that of the working-class child with unskilled father, large family and poor housing.

The National Association for Remedial Education has published a report on adult illiteracy which documents the history of 1,126 adults who were receiving some form of reading instruction.[7] About half of these known illiterates were considered by their teachers to be of average intelligence or above. 46 per cent of those assessed had reading ages of less than seven years, that is, they would not be able to read a popular newspaper, road signs, hoardings or public instructions—and they could not write a simple note. The students themselves considered that the chief cause of their failure was inadequate teaching. Their replies indicated boredom, apathy and a wholesale rejection of the form of education to which they had been subjected :

'I didn't do anything at school. I just sat.'
'I hated the same old routine.'
'I always took Friday off.'

What Can be Done?

It is a fearful indictment of our educational system that significant numbers of pupils *of normal intellectual capacity* pass completely through it without acquiring even a basis of literacy. How can it happen? People will not believe one when told that there are boys and girls, not mentally retarded, who have entered and left secondary schools without being able to read.

With all the evidence about the vital importance of the early years, the case for a root and branch approach through increased nursery provision hardly requires to be made. An early start, with considerable emphasis on the development of language skills, offers the best hope of preparing children for a more successful school career. It is not sensible to expect quick progress, or a sudden reversal of previous learning patterns, however. Rather, the aim should be to achieve continuity of procedures throughout the whole primary school life of the pupil. A friendly, informal learning situation must be coupled to a systematic ('structured') introduction to the complex process of learning to read : a difficult balance to strike, but an essential one. To offset the effects of pupil mobility, more sophisticated and detailed record cards are desirable and some means has to be found of making this information available to the class teacher. Stability of staff is highly desirable but continuity can be achieved without it, if the person in charge has a well-developed scheme of work. The Schools Council's *Breakthrough to Literacy* material has been a major contribution and its widespread use in schools with literacy problems would surely help to provide a structure for the reading instruction without impinging too heavily upon the child-centred atmosphere which is so much admired by American visitors to English primary schools. One knows many schools where all the problems exist in abundance and yet morale is high, the children are literate, interested and progressing. The burning question is, why some schools and not others? The answer most commonly given has been : the quality of the head. No one would dispute the importance of good leadership in difficult circumstances; it is one of the 'variables' which research workers find difficult to isolate. Thus, Peaker has pointed out that 'there is much in the situation which the observations have been unable to grasp, such as variations in native wit, in ambition and in teaching. . . .'[8] Indeed a third of the total variation in the 1968 achievement figures remained unexplained. This unexplained variance offers teachers a ray of hope. 'The general tenor of the report is to illustrate the importance of the early stages for all that comes after. Well begun is half done. But, of course, only half. Nothing in the evidence detracts from the importance of secondary education.'[9]

If secondary schools are prepared to accept whole-heartedly the fact that boys and girls of very low educational attainment will be included in every new intake, it becomes possible to arrange for suitable instruction to be given. Certainly, it is never too late, even after years of failure, to make a fresh start. Though the task becomes more difficult with every passing year, remedial education, properly conceived, can be undertaken at any age. I have set out elsewhere[10] the kind of approach which is likely to bring success. It is not proposed to restate principles well-known to teachers of reading, only to emphasize that techniques exist in abundance, so that illiteracy among pupils of normal ability is inexcusable and needless. Only a very small proportion of those who fail have a specific learning disability of sufficient intensity to explain their failure in reading; all the rest, given adequate teaching can be helped.

The boredom to which the adult illiterates referred has much to do with their failure in school. The curriculum for slow learners in secondary schools tends to be very narrowly based. They are often denied access to interesting experiences—in Science, for example—because they have difficulty in reading instructions and results. Progressive secondary schools are showing how these handicaps can be overcome. Much of the note-taking can be done verbally, using cassette tape recorders. Very simple answer sheets can be prepared, using diagrams and simple Yes/No choices. (Two Schools Council projects have been given tasks in this field.) There is no doubt that secondary schools can stimulate and hold the attention of difficult adolescents.[11]

Community Involvement

It might be felt that to confine discussion to what can be attempted in the schools themselves is to be hopelessly superficial; that the roots of educational failure have gone too deep for anything less than 'a comprehensive social movement towards community development and community redevelopment' of which even an Educational Priority Area (let alone a school) would constitute only one part. There is some truth in this, but the part that a secondary school can play in helping to regenerate a neighbourhood is quite considerable. In any case, no such community redevelopment is in sight for most areas, so that the community must start with the school itself, or nowhere.

Dr Halsey's EPA project has produced numerous examples of the ways in which school and community can be brought into fruitful communication. The Coventry Community Development Project has begun to show signs of genuine innovation, with a very active and well-researched social education programme linked to a school which seems to have offered parents the opportunity for active involvement. At Telford, Shropshire, many of the amenities of a new town have been incorporated in the school campus, so that public and pupils share swimming baths, a theatre, playing fields and so on. As well as affording the pupils magnificent amenities, this set-up brings parents and others into the ambit of the school in a meaningful way. All too often, 'community schools' have been little more than buildings attended only by invitation, for 'open evenings' to see children's work, or for the occasional musical production. The Telford community school gives adults a genuine reason for visiting the school premises and the prospect of enjoying themselves while they are there. When more activities are centred in school buildings there can be more *casual* contact between parents and teachers, and a better teacher/parent relationship can only benefit the life of the school and the community as a whole.

Parental interest and support is vitally important to the success of a school, but it can only operate effectively where the basic aim and atmosphere of the school is one of providing adequately for each and every one of its pupils.

NOTES

1 *Cross'd With Adversity*, Schools Council Working Paper 27 (Evans/ Methuen, 1970).

2 Central Advisory Council for Education (England), *Half Our Future* (HMSO, 1963).

3 In 'Lessons Learnt', *Remedial Education* 4, 2 (1969), pp. 92–4.

4 Ibid. pp. 92–4.

5 Reva Lincoln, *Interviews for Birmingham Educational Priority Area Project* (unpublished).

6 *Cross'd With Adversity* (see 1 above).

7 *Adult Illiteracy* (National Association for Remedial Education, 1972).

8 G. F. Peaker, *The Plowden Children Four Years Later* (National Foundation for Educational Research, 1971).

9 Ibid. p. 7.

10 Paul Widlake, *Literacy in the Secondary School* (National Association for Remedial Education, 1972).

11 For an example of the way in which this can be achieved, see *Remedial Education*, 7, 3 (1972).

BILL KIRKPATRICK

Protest and Poverty: Drug Abuse and the Young

When young people take to drugs, they are expressing deep dissatisfaction with their lives, both on a personal level and within society as a whole. Conflict between the young and the rest of society is not new—young people must always react against outdated educational, social and political structures if creative change in society is to be achieved. Every age has feared its youth, for they are the symbols of change. In our own age, however, the protests of the young have taken spectacular forms as they strive to forge an identity for themselves within a society that seems bent on depersonalization and materialism, upon creating what Patrick Golding calls 'the Broilerhouse Society'.[1]

Some young people have turned increasingly to violence, others have joined specific groups like the hippy movement, while a growing number protest by dropping out altogether. In doing this they reject the values they see in society, and seek new standards of freedom, truth and love. They want complete freedom to be themselves and to welcome *all* experiences unconditionally. They are prepared to live what Rosemary Haughton calls 'the knife edge of experience'[2] and this often means choosing a life of poverty. In this, and in their search for a more authentic expression of truth and love than what they find around them, they can be called Christ-like. This 'integrity of purpose', as we may call it, can link them with Christians at work in the fields of prevention and after-care among drug takers.

Another link between young drug takers and those trying to help them has been the growth of a Christian presence within the Underground drug culture itself. As the Reverend Kenneth Leech says :

This has taken a variety of forms, from the radical, liberated church groups in the United States to the charismatic Jesus people and a variety of Jesus communes and Jesus freaks. But perhaps the most interesting and most subtly elusive element is the perceptible revival of interest in Christian mysticism. It was inevitable, as psychedelic drugs gave way to non-chemical approaches to consciousness, that at some stage someone would stumble upon the vast tradition of Christian mysticism and contemplative prayer. Nor is it surprising that those Christians who have made most impact on the drug scene have been those who have held firm to their 'deposit of faith' and have not lost a grip on their own spirituality, be they Pentecostalist preachers or contemplative nuns. Indeed, one of the most frequently heard complaints from young hippies about clergymen is that they do not talk enough about God.[3]

In this context, drug abuse can be seen as a protest against the spiritual poverty of materialism through the chemically-induced 'God trip'. Unfortunately there can be no 'instant heaven', no ready-mixed revelation. Mystics, gurus and holy men of the past have insisted upon a period of preparation for the state of revelation; 'the dark night of the soul' is no empty phrase. It is entirely different from the dark night of depression, just as ignorance of spiritual matters is different from 'The Cloud of Unknowing'. There is no short cut to Parnassus. Young people who are not prepared to take the hard way of prayer and meditation are not able to cope with the lurid dreams induced by LSD, and the 'God trip' has proved disastrous for many, frequently leading to complete mental disintegration.

When we talk of 'poverty' we should imply more than the 'poverty of materialism' which many recognize around us. We are all involved in the basic human situation where we experience the poverty both of those who desperately need love and those who attempt, out of *their* need, to give it. These two, the negative and positive forms of poverty, are held together by the law of love. Again and again one is forced to return to the fact that love is the basic law, the only creative force, the very source of life. Young people, like most of us, are searching for an authentic love, and it is in this context of need that we should now consider some aspects of the social background to the misuse and abuse of drugs.

In the current discussion of the drug problem we should not forget that drug taking, and indeed many other facets of the so-called 'permissive society', are not new. Colin McInnes calls to mind George and Weedon Grossmith's *The Diary of a Nobody*, published in 1870, in which we are told of the man who

> throws up his job in a bank, wears extraordinary clothing, speaks an incomprehensible jargon, makes peculiar friends, consorts with dubious females, is mad about show-biz, fiddles successfully on the Stock Exchange, and rapidly takes off for ever, leaving his parents lamenting vanished stabilities of an earlier generation. *Violence*—one never dared to walk in the Seven Dials, let alone east of Aldgate Pump. *Drugs*—there are endless references in late Victorian letters and memoirs to doses of laudanum and other opium derivatives. In late Victorian days there were far more addicts than there are today, but they did not know they were addicts. *Sexual permissiveness*—prostitution in Victorian England was on such an enormous and blatant scale that all foreign observers remarked on it. The abundance of harlots, coupled with gross overcrowding and the defencelessness of girls in service or in factories, positively invited sex unlimited. Seduction of children was commonplace. *Pornography*—was readily available and indeed more fully available than today.[4] (My italics.)

Can we expect different behaviour today when people are still living in overcrowded cities under conditions of even greater stress?

Drug abuse should not be seen as an isolated problem. It stems from a mass of individual and environmental inadequacies. We need to be aware that nearly all drugs being misused are drugs which *alter the state of mind*. It is inevitable that people who find themselves constantly dissatisfied with their 'normal' existence will try these in an attempt to improve their condition. It must be recognized that these people are the casualties of the system which created them, a system which demands (among other things) that young people succeed academically or commercially within a specific period of time if they are not to be classified as second-class citizens. For those who are unable to protest outwardly against such a system, drugs act as a neutralizer of anxiety and are often used to mask insecurity. For some, drugs offer a way of putting their problems into cold-storage, as it were, until they feel strong enough to cope with them. Others take drugs to ward off impending mental breakdown or as an aid towards controlling their own aggression. Many youngsters who are in contact with drug users do not themselves become addicted. For those who do go on from 'soft' drugs such as pep-pills and barbiturates to 'hard' drugs such as heroin and cocaine, their weapon of protest has become a weapon of self-destruction.

Any understanding of the drug abuser must develop from the recognition of the addict within each one of us, as an inner compelling force, ever present and threatening. One reason for the growing and almost morbid fascination of the subject for the public, whether expressed as fear or sympathy, may be that the addict mirrors our own socially-acceptable and quite legal addictions. Which of us, for instance, is not addicted to tea, coffee, alcohol, cigarettes, sex, or television? Drug dependence, irrespective of type, is the misuse of whatever it is upon which we may have become dependent. Is not our concern for the drug user based on our inner consciousness that he is an enlarged reflection of our own desire to retreat into a synthetic existence?

The drug abuser, then, is a person who, for reasons usually unknown to himself, has adopted a system of values and an outlook on life that make his behaviour contrary to that which his particular community would label as 'normal'. For this reason we might classify him as a sociopath. Within this subculture will be found the constitutionally weak, the frustrated, the emotionally unstable, the inadequate personality, the schizoid personality, the paranoid and the psychopath. (To label all drug abusers as psychopaths is wrong, for there are no more within this group than there are in other minority groups.) Whatever label we attach, it is essential to realize that when we say, 'John is an addict', what we are in fact saying is that 'addict' is only *one* of the things that John is. This leaves room for the 'persona' of John to be recognized, quite apart from his addiction.

Socially sick as this person is, he is usually held in such low esteem that few persons within the 'enabling professions', whether state or voluntary, are prepared to be and to work alongside him. Such negative attitudes occur because addiction is regarded as a vice leading to the progressive moral deterioration not only of the individual but also of the community. In associating the drug abuser with all sorts of crime, we are perhaps being provided with a morally convenient scapegoat. Is the drug abuser the unwitting sacrificial victim of our age? Is he a sign that we are fast forgetting that men are after all human and may only remain so for as long as we pay attention to each other as persons?

The 'drug problem' is a disease which is reflected in the whole of our society, and in each addicted person we can see society's illnesses represented. Basically there appear to be three main groups of young people affected.

There is the young person, often from a socially deprived area, who has had difficulty with his education. Having failed the selection examination at eleven, he will have left school at fifteen and will have had many jobs. He is usually a member of a delinquent group and will have had perhaps several encounters with the law. Despite the fact that his family life may be disrupted because of his delinquency pattern, he is usually well integrated into his family and neighbourhood. His drug taking is only part of a particular attitude and pattern of life which he shares with his family and friends. It has largely replaced the drinking habit which was the placebo of an earlier generation, and may be a continuation of an already established delinquency pattern.

A second group contains the boy or girl from middle-class suburbia who has probably begun higher education. These young people are seldom seen before the courts, but they are often in conflict with their parents and involved in various protest movements. For them drug taking is an act of initiation into one of the many 'truth-seeking' groups which, for them, has replaced the home as a source of security and identification. But as they become more and more alienated from their families they become vulnerable and easy prey for the drug pusher. For these, drug abuse is mainly a gesture of non-conformity to the tradition of their elders.

A third group is made up of drifters : young people who drift all over the country, usually ending up in one of the larger cities such as London, Manchester, Liverpool or Glasgow. They are attracted to the large conurbations because of the anonymity and freedom from social restraints offered there. They tend to gravitate to the café/club culture and are often without friends or money, constantly on the move to nowhere in particular. These folk represent a small and vulnerable group who are often very disturbed mentally. They present the most difficult of problems, as they reject all forms of social, medical or psychiatric help.

The care of the drug-dependent person hinges upon a combination of intense personal and community care. One without the other weakens our efforts as the drug abuser moves toward treatment, towards rehabilitation. Our concern, therefore, demands that we offer a *comprehensive* approach to his very personal problem (*our* social problem) through the co-ordinated efforts of the national health and social services of the State, alongside those of the legal and voluntary organizations. We must take into consideration that man is a complex inter-relationship of physical, mental, social and spiritual factors, which cannot be understood except in terms of their interaction. Therefore any comprehensive approach must begin where it must end, with the person in the community.

During the early part of 1967 sixteen treatment centres were set up in and around London. These centres are meant to be the *focal point of first encounter* in the continuing process of rehabilitation. The patient/staff relationship is all-important, if the addict is to be successfully weaned off drugs and enabled to face life without them. To illustrate the approach described in the paragraph above, I should like to quote from my practical experience of being involved in the setting up of such a service in the East End of London. This is not to suggest that we were more successful than other treatment centres, for there are as many ways of caring for the drug-dependent person as there are such persons. While the same philosophy of care has been maintained from the beginning, some practical changes have occurred since 1969.

Since the centre opened, approximately 300 individuals claiming to be on drugs (255 males and 45 females) have received treatment. Of the whole group, 250 were taking heroin in combination with some other drug, usually cocaine or methedrine, although the latter has since been removed from the market. The majority of those attending the clinic were between seventeen and twenty-three years old. An average of 100 patients per week were seen regularly by appointment, in addition to those referred to us from other agencies. 90 of these were male, 10 female; 65 were local and 35 came in from other districts. 59 of the local boys and two of the local girls were living at home; in this way they differed from those outside the immediate neighbourhood of the clinic. At that time, 36 patients were taking part in various kinds of group activities. Approximately 50 per cent of the patients were working fulltime and for many of these we had evening clinics. The rest worked rather spasmodically, when not in detention centres, remand homes, borstals, prisons or general hospitals (the latter as a result of infection from using dirty needles and syringes rather than from the side effects of the drug itself).

The largest number of unemployed were from outside the area and many appeared to be unemployable. We had three married couples (both husband and wife addicted) and eight married couples where one or other partner was addicted. We had six pairs of brothers who were addicted. It is interesting to note that although this centre was in the East End of London, with a large Jewish population, only two Jewish boys were in need of treatment. Up to 1969 there were no coloured persons among our patients. This is contrary to what one is led to believe by sensational newspaper reports. The strong pattern of family life and a close-knit community feeling, often supported by a strong religious tradition, are potent factors in keeping these young people from drifting into the drug scene.

Most of the patients followed a poly-addiction pattern, i.e., that of being dependent upon more than one drug : they tended to over-emphasize the amount of heroin being taken and underestimate the amount of other drugs. It is essential to remember this when admitting the person to a casualty, general or medical ward or to prison. The largest percentage of those living in the East End appeared to have started on pills of the amphetamine type because of group pressures or for social reasons. Most had tried cannabis, though few had taken it regularly, so far as we were able to assess this. Those outside the area tended to take larger amounts of heroin and were more consistent users of cannabis.

The sharing of 'gear', that is of needles and syringes including the disposable type, is fairly common. Most 'fix', that is give themselves an injection, either by 'skin popping' (intermuscular) or by

'mainlining' (intravenously). The patients fix two to six times daily
on the average, initially as soon as the chemist opens in the morning, and last thing at night, either before going home in the evening
or just before dropping off to sleep. Between fixes, the unemployed
addict wanders around looking for friends and for drugs, and he
may eventually fix from sheer boredom. For many there is a fascination in the act of fixing. Some fix alone, others like an audience.
Some may take up to half an hour, so ritualized is the act. The
needle and syringe appear to have taken the place of personal
relationships. For some it is a help towards socializing with friends.
Some appear to be addicted to the needle rather than to any
specific drug. A great many are prepared to inject anything into
their veins : amphetamines, barbiturates, tobacco juice, whisky or
any other substance, which again suggests that the addiction is to
the needle rather than to the drug.

Each patient will have come to the clinic of his own free will,
initially to get drugs on the cheap and to legalize his taking of
drugs, especially heroin. He is not given the drug immediately but
must first become registered. A specimen of urine is collected. This
is followed by a lengthy noting of his history with special emphasis
on his drug and social histories. This is then verified from as many
sources as possible, beginning with the Home Office and any other
legal, medical, social or educational establishments known to have
been in contact with the patient. Initially the desire for a 'cure', that
is treatment, is practically nil. However those of us involved in this
sphere of concern are convinced that unless the drug abuser desires
of his own accord to come off drugs, he will not do so, whether
forced by his wife, family, medical, legal, social or religious pressures.
Only those persons highly motivated and supported will go through
the hell of a physical and psychological withdrawal.

The immediate concern for all of us involved within the caring
processes of the community must be directed towards the re-enforc-
ing of any *positive* attempts to come off drugs. This will occur for
several reasons : one suspects that a person will come off drugs when
he no longer feels insecure, when he is no longer afraid of facing
life without drugs. Treatment begins by helping the person to
change his attitude of 'once a junkie, always a junkie'. And we shall
only be able to do this when *we* understand the *why* of drug abuse,
when we can appreciate the socio-psychological and medical aspects

of this social disease. Only then will we see the addict as a sick member of our society.

All caring personnel must be prepared to work with the addict's family, in the knowledge that drug abuse is very often the result of non-relationship within the family and the community. If we are to assist the drug abuser towards a more creative way of life, we will need to assess the community's attitudes and values. These and these alone will determine the policies which will bring about the easing of this problem. We have to decide *as a community* to treat it as a health problem needing all the financial, legal, medical, social and spiritual resources that we devote to other community problems. Only then will sufficient funds be allocated for initiating treatment and research programmes.

The essential criteria for evaluating the effectiveness of any treatment programme are the subsequent behaviour of the addict and his re-absorption into the community. The question of which treatment is best in dealing with drug abusers should not arise if we regard *all* methods as part of the total community approach. There are perhaps as many different avenues of cure as there are motivations for wanting a cure, especially when we realize that the drug-dependent population is a heterogeneous community, a subculture composed of persons of varying qualities, attitudes and motivations. It is essential to realize that there is no such person as 'the classic junkie'.

For the most part drug dependency tends to be a chronic relapsing condition, yet the person who relapses should not be considered any more of a failure than the person who requires repeated treatments for recurring medical, surgical or psychiatric conditions. It is because of this tendency to relapse that the patient will have to be followed up in the community for an extended period before treatment may be considered successful. This may be between five and seven years. Our attitudes to care might alter if we were to consider these persons as belonging to a new group of the young, chronically sick.

We found it essential at our centre for all caring personnel to be prepared to work within a flexible situation. The selection of personnel, whether professional or non-professional, should be on the basis of their high frustration-tolerance and their ability to listen. These two qualities are of paramount importance in creating therapeutically sound relationships. Anyone who has ever worked with drug-dependent persons will know that frustrations are numerous. Therefore personnel must be objective, optimistic and prepared to vary their approach and treatment in individual cases. In short, they need to be committed to the *person* behind the mask of addiction, and for an indefinite period.

Most of us within the 'enabling', the 'personal' professions are stimulated towards others by our own basic needs, and by the response and concern shown towards us by those to whom we are directing our concern. In this particular sphere, however, we must expect to offer all and to receive little if anything in return. This is one caring situation where our need for the patient is overruled by his need for us. Our central point of concern should be, what is wrong with him as a person? We can encourage a less rigid attitude towards him if we regard him as having been pushed out rather than as having dropped out from society.

The prevention of drug addiction is more than a matter of lecturing, writing or even working in this field. It means a deliberate effort by the community as a whole to aid in the elimination of all the social conditions which encourage the depersonalization of the individual. We can begin by asking what kind of a society or non-society it is that produces this sociopathic personality, and aim at encouraging anything which helps another individual towards the fullness of living through and for others.

Through our united concern, whether as Christians or not, we must help everyone to share equally in the fullness of life : the possession of full physical, mental, social and spiritual health. The success of any 'enabling ministry' is linked to its capacity to assume and maintain a truly human dimension, its capacity to understand what lies behind the youth protest movements of today. However much we might like to clear the streets of people who protest, or to put them away on an island or in prison, we cannot. Nor can we divide the mystical body of Christ by cutting off the man or woman who uses a needle in his arm as an act of protest. We can never rid ourselves of that man or woman, because we have a responsibility to be there with him. The clergy especially have a direct and inescapable responsibility for the care and cure of souls.

We must not only ask what the community can do for us, but rather what we can do for our brother, who protests in a way that not only diminishes him but ourselves. In realizing this, we become aware of the fact that 'we burn the candle of our lives through each other.'[5]

NOTES

1 Patrick Golding, *The Broilerhouse Society* (Lesley Frewin, 1969).

2 Rosemary Haughton, *The Knife Edge of Experience* (Darton, Longman & Todd, 1972).

3 Rev. Kenneth Leech, 'Christianity and Drugs', *The Times* (9 October, 1972).

4 Colin McInnes, 'A Confusing Choice', *The Times* (14 November, 1970).

5 See Theo Westow, *Who Is My Brother?* (Sheed & Ward, 1968).

JOHN WILDER

Mental Illness: Its Relation to Poverty in Urban Societies

The term 'the new poor' sometimes used nowadays can be misleading. The new poor are only new to those discovering them for the first time. The poor—that is, those with the least money and who suffer from severe personal and social deprivation—tend to congregate, as they always have done, in the twilight areas of cities; many are additionally impoverished through disablement, both physical and psychological, either genetically or environmentally based. Such persons are sometimes hindered by their own low expectations, and their acceptance of bad living conditions. Indeed, twilight areas can be defined as those parts of our cities where inferior quality is accepted as part of the way of life, and where poverty permeates the whole fabric of the environment. These inferior standards embrace living conditions, education, work—the totality of life experience. The poor are those with no choice. When individuals emerge through these difficulties to a more satisfactory way of life, they are invariably seen as exceptional persons, whereas they usually represent the norm for the rest of society. These twilight environments desperately require the very best that society can offer; they usually achieve only the mediocre which, by comparison, looks better than it is.

Whilst there exists a genteel poor—that is, those who live in a middle-class community with an income well below the level maintained by their class—the real poverty is where it has always been, in the twilight areas, the decaying communities, where some observers discover a happy unity amongst the 'have-nots'. It may be true that wealth does not bring happiness, but neither does poverty. High-density living and poverty produce sad conflicts within such communities, which tend to become havens for the weary and the anonymous, where a process of conditioning erodes initiative or the ambition to leave. These areas tend to be places where industrialization, the exploitation of labour and neglect by governments have led to severe deterioration of the environment and of social conditions. They also have roads, grossly inadequate for the needs of commercial traffic, which are noisy and contribute greatly to the pollution of the atmosphere. There is usually a legacy of substandard houses, many of which are unfit for human habitation, and of industrial and commercial slums. Generally the areas are crying out for redevelopment, which is being tackled piecemeal at a rate determined by several factors, not the least of which is the cost of government loans and the repayment of previous ones.

Since the Second World War, there has been some progress towards redevelopment and rehousing, but owing to the length of time taken to complete some of the schemes, the earlier post-war developments are growing old and are beginning to have a depressing effect on the more recent additions to the schemes. Thus, the twilight areas are like growing cancers in the body of society, perpetuating and isolating themselves until, finally, piecemeal solutions are found to be useless and far-reaching social surgery and rehabilitation become necessary.

When we reflect upon the problems of the poor we recognize that they tend to lack three major assets : wealth, health and opportunity. The mentally ill are one group who are generally denied the financial means of achieving a satisfactory life style, and this is particularly true in the twilight areas. There is certainly much scope for improvement of disability pensions to provide basic needs. Money in this context is regarded as security; in fact, the department that manages such matters carries the name 'Social Security'. But money alone is not the answer; real social security is to be sought in our environment, our homes and our relationships, not in pensions.

The importance of the quality of the environment is recognized by governments and demonstrated by their attempts to build model living conditions for people resettled in the country, in the new towns. These were planned as a means of lowering population density in the blighted urban areas. But selection for living accommodation in a new town is basically dependent upon the wage-earner possessing a skill required by local industry, and a stable work record, both good recommendations for employment in a new area. Thus, a social syphon has been evolved through which the young, ambitious, able, imaginative members are attracted away from the old communities.

In terms of mental health, new towns are an obvious improvement upon the twilight areas. Looking at the very limited research on this subject we discover that mental illness requiring hospital admission in a new town was 52 per cent below the expected rate, based on national figures,[1] whereas for a decaying part of London it was 77 per cent above the national rate.[2] A government report on housing in Greater London itself referred to living conditions in a twilight area as follows :

> The herding together of people, often incompatible, the inconveniences, the lack of space . . . the inadequate and inconvenient washing, sanitary and food handling facilities, stairs, noise . . . the dirt, dilapidation and depressing appearances consequent upon the neglect of parts used in common, all have their effect. To these must be added the increased liability to have home accidents, infections, contagion, risk of fire, and mental stress. It is impossible to assess the relative incidence of different types of illness as a result of bad housing. On the other hand, various analyses of applications for rehousing on medical grounds have shown the preponderance of two concomitants of multiple occupation—respiratory illness and psychological or psychosomatic disorders.[3]

Obviously, the physical environment has an immediate impact on people, and in particular on their morale. The statistics can give no adequate impression of the drab surroundings in which they may have to live—despite the progress which has been made in slum clearance.

Attempts to involve the Government in a study of the incidence of mental illness, particularly in relation to the environment in which the mentally ill live, have been ignored or parried for some time[4] until a recent Minister at the Department of Health and Social Security, Mr Richard Crossman, agreed that this should be done,[5] and his Urban Development Programme now gives some power to concentrate on the black spots. The criteria for defining black spots are based on multi-deprivation, which shows itself,[6] for example, in notable deficiencies in the physical environment, particularly poor housing, over-crowding, above average-size families, persistent unemployment, a high proportion of children in trouble or in need of care, and a substantial degree of immigrant settlement. Our own studies[7] confirm that it is in such environments that high incidence of mental illness requiring urgent hospitalization occurs. (Our current research shows that it is possible to predict with 95 per cent accuracy the incidence of schizophrenia in urban societies. What is particularly significant is the fact that the key data is (i) percentage of total employable population unemployed; (ii) percentage of male workers in unskilled work; (iii) percentage of people living alone; (iv) percentage of people living with more than $1\frac{1}{2}$ persons per room and (v) gross density (persons per acre including open spaces).

We frequently hear the activists of public opinion recite that one in six women and one in nine men will become mentally ill in their lifetime. This suggests that, selected at random, almost anyone could become mentally ill. The truth of the matter is that the likelihood of becoming mentally ill is higher if we live in an area of high unemployment, overcrowding and high density. The following table shows this clearly.

SCHIZOPHRENIC PATIENTS DISCHARGED IN ONE YEAR

Town	Predicted per 10,000 adult population	Vulnerable district	Predicted per 10,000 adult population
Glasgow	23.15	Glasgow Central	41.20
Liverpool	16.59	Liverpool Exchange	26.32
Sunderland	15.67	—	
Newcastle	15.46	Newcastle Central	21.40
South Shields	15.23	—	
Aberdeen	15.06	Aberdeen North	16.97
Manchester	14.47	Manchester Exchange	18.48
Middlesborough	14.41	—	
Rhondda	14.11	Rhondda East	14.49
Blackpool	14.05	Blackpool North	14.45
Cardiff	13.47	—	

NB National figures: 10 per 10,000 adult population.

SOURCE: PRA Research Unit 1966 Census (Regional Hospital Boards Office of Population Census and Surveys, 1972).

Whereas the appallingly high figures of national incidence of psychiatric patients in need of hospital treatment are in themselves revealing, they give no adequate indication of the considerable numbers in mental distress within our community. For a long time we have blinkered ourselves to the plight of the senile, the alcoholic (there seems to be even less tolerance for the alcoholic who drinks unrefined spirits), the disturbed adolescent who manifests his disturbance by becoming a drug addict, vandal or drop-out, and the bereaved and unsuccessful, many of whom manifest their maladjustment in ways which cause discomfort to themselves and to those around them.

Stress is often said by the successful to be 'character-forming'. But excessive stress can well result in instability and a further deterioration of environmental conditions. The 'battered baby' syndrome, and the considerable number of children taken into care, indicate that excessive stress can lead to a sick and divided community. The so-called group cohesion of low-income groups is now a myth which shows some semblance of validity only when—and this is seldom the case—the people concerned realize that there is nothing to lose and go into the attack. Ulster is, perhaps, an example of this. But generally the picture is one of apathy. Drastic and desperate community programmes are required to try to rekindle unity, idealism and leadership among the poor if they are to undertake a battle waged less against capitalism than against central and local government mediocrity.

It is important not to regard the mentally ill as a new phenomenon. Mental illness appears to be the price we pay for 'civilization'. I suspect that the more we examine poverty the more we shall find that mental illness is a major cause and consequence of the various other poverties, and that it occurs where any of the essentials of life, not least love, are missing. However, the increasing organization of our society, the observation and measurement of things, people and performance, gives us a greater awareness of shortcomings, and brings blemishes in society constantly into focus. Efficiency in organization demands perfection and ultimately leads to rejection of the imperfect. Automation and the use of computers may accelerate this process. Organized society, with its rules and controls, brings with it provisions for those who can conform. Those who cannot conform will be distressed. The mentally ill are in the midst of this dilemma. They have a vital need for self-expression but fear the society which contains them. Those who do not fit into the organized pattern, especially if they do not have private means, are regarded as deviants or inadequates and are ignored for as long as possible. The many odd corners of employment into which they used to fit—casual roadwork, work as a night watchman, and so on, are diminishing. As mechanization develops, the unskilled and uneducated are needed less. Furthermore, as the disabled increase in numbers and years, so their employment possibilities diminish still further, and those that rely on government aid or fixed incomes for their standard of living will depend on annual increases linked with the rising cost of living.

Bearing in mind the fact that the more stress a community is compelled to suffer, the higher the incidence of mental illness within it, we can see that to treat a mentally ill person with drugs alone is to evade the basic problem that his illness was probably caused by the quality of his life outside the hospital, and that is unchanged by his medical treatment. Life for anyone, particularly the mentally ill, must contain promise of hope. Prolonged poverty permeates all aspects of life and erodes all that it encompasses, including hope.

One of the developments of drug therapy is concerned with enabling patients not to react to the stress of their environment with bizarre behaviour. The new drugs subdue these symptoms. There is a great drive now to develop drugs which do not depend upon the patient's co-operation in consuming them every few hours, but which by a single injection will maintain their effect over many weeks. This is excellent progress, but we must find ways of enriching the patient's life with more than chemicals. It was Thomas Carlyle who said : 'Brothers, I am sorry I have got no pill for curing the maladies of society.' Whilst the relief of immediate suffering must be paramount and is to be applauded, the psychotrophic drugs only increase tolerance to stress, or relieve the symptoms which occur under stress. Perhaps the medical and ancillary services concentrate on preserving this level of progress, hoping that other members of society will concern themselves with the quality of the environment itself. But so far as the mentally ill are concerned, improvement in environmental conditions is less likely because (a) they are less able to express their needs in words; (b) many without families in an area tend not to settle there long to await dispensation of subsidized accommodation, and (c) the 'image' of the psychiatric patient in the public mind still deters co-operation.

Schizophrenic patients, particularly the unmarried, are regarded as being a group most in need of intensive after-care. They tend to be most susceptible to environmental conditions and to drift down the social scale so that poverty is caused by their lack of ability to cope when ill.[8] The sad thing is that much of such mental illness is intermittent, so that being well may also mean awareness of social failure and disappointment with life. A study of 174 schizophrenic patients discharged from hospital in East London showed that a third lived in sub-standard housing, that 55 per cent were unemployed (excluding housewives), and that 54 per cent had no friends. The most significant disclosure, however, was that of all the patients discharged in East London in one year, 45 per cent were not traceable. These were all chronic patients. We might well ask ourselves how much poverty amongst the mentally ill goes unobserved and how far the connection between the two is unrecognized or ignored.

It is the element of choice in directing one's own life which nurtures human imagination and morale. Expectations of the future motivate us towards effort which brings its rewards. The more our freedom of expression is reduced, the more damaging the impact on our mental processes. When trapped in social conditions which produce despair and offer no hope, one is eventually left with a final choice between acceptance or suicide. It is, then, understandable that the majority of those chronic mentally ill living in poverty, especially those without adequate community care, make no progress.

Social experiments by the Psychiatric Rehabilitation Association showed that indignation rather than acceptance was an activating force leading to hope and improved morale. When patients resented their lot, they became concerned with change and became responsive to self-help in association with others. Such militancy is viewed with much suspicion by those seeking for these people a placid acceptance through a pill or palliative. It is almost a social philosophy to say 'we cannot afford to give them a better society, so let us reduce their (and our) awareness of it.' Perhaps it is the class gulf separating the social organizers from the have-nots which prevents the former recognizing that democracy is therapeutic even if it is less convenient than bureaucracy.

Recognizing that poverty and mental illness exclude one from life, PRA worked for over ten years on this problem, involving patients, ex-patients, relatives and friends in planning and building their own rehabilitation programmes. As a result, they have quietly and sometimes not so quietly influenced communities to make significant provisions for the mentally ill and they have developed a comprehensive range of facilities including a number of day centres, industrial units, evening centres, a residential centre and group homes; and they have initiated research which is influencing government and local authority attitudes. This project arose out of the need to combat despair. Involvement dispersed apathy; success generated optimism. Dignity blossomed where a purpose in life evolved. But the success belonged to everyone, in particular the patients who played a positive role throughout. Their involvement has been the therapy that has taught them that they have a right to better standards, and ways of achieving them.

But although this experiment has involved over 6,000 patients, it barely touches the total problem. Vast numbers of people in mental distress live in our decaying communities, unknown to the statisticians. Their condition does not make them vocal. General Practitioners and social workers know many of them and they write letters, fruitlessly, to local government officials requesting simple facilities such as housing and employment, mainly because they want the patient to know that they are trying to help. But seldom does the effort go beyond this. Very few doctors or social workers will take forceful action to try to influence major changes in the interest of their patients or clients. Is this because it takes time and they are overworked? Or because it means 'knocking' the establishment and this might affect their livelihoods? Or because the need for establishing priorities means giving first aid rather than becoming involved in prevention? There is a strange blockage which prevents the small army of informed workers getting at the real problem in society.

Fortunately, a new development is quietly having effect in schools in areas of poverty. Under the nondescript title of 'Social Studies' real preventive work is emerging. The subject might equally be described as mental or social hygiene. Youngsters, particularly academic failures of which the twilight areas have the greater numbers, are being taught to understand and manipulate their environment instead of the reverse. They are learning that they too have rights and can play an effective, responsible role in raising standards for themselves and others who are worse off. I have great hopes for this approach which, applied as part of our basic education, must lead to better mental and social health.

Poverty and mental illness are none the less thoroughly integrated into the administrative order of things. Our mental hospitals are old, inadequate, over-crowded buildings. Nearly half of all hospital beds are occupied by mentally ill or mentally subnormal patients, but the daily cost of their care is dramatically lower than for the care of other hospital patients—barely a quarter of total inpatient costs.[9] Much of the large discrepancy in standards between psychiatric and general hospitals has persisted through the years since the days when psychiatric institutions were intended only to contain the disturbed patients rejected by the community, whereas the general hospital (a short-stay institution) has needed to keep in step with the normal expectations of the community. It is also apparent that while there have been improvements in interior decoration and in creating space in many psychiatric wards, the social class distribution of patients tends to give better conditions to middle-class patients. There are many explanations or denials of this trend, but the fact remains that those who aspire to middle-class standards relate more effectively to the medical staff, since culturally and socially they tend to speak the same language.

Obviously, not all the poor are mentally ill, but they have a greater chance, statistically, of becoming so. Not all the mentally ill are poor, but unless they have private incomes there is again a high likelihood of their becoming so; the two conditions go together. Real effort is needed urgently to halt the process : we are developing in our cities ghettos of unemployable, unwanted people, for whom life offers so little that unreality is preferable. Is this effort too much to ask in an age of affluence and technological brilliance?

There is much comment, written, filmed and discussed, on the subject of society and its casualties, but it is seldom made by those in the fray. Whilst there is obviously a role for the commentators and for publicity in tackling the problem, real leadership must be discovered at the grass-roots level; this is also where true community development must begin. Perhaps the real task ahead is to educe such leadership, and to teach dissatisfaction with the gross inequalities that exist, even if this upsets the *status quo*.

NOTES

1 L. Taylor and S. Chave, *Mental Health and Environment* (Longman, 1964).

2 *Mental Health of East London* (Psychiatric Rehabilitation Association, 1966).

3 Milner Holland, *Report on Housing in Greater London* (HMSO, 1965).

4 Kenneth Robinson (*Hansard*, June 1967).

5 Richard Crossman (*Hansard*, July, 1969).

6 *A Major Experiment in Improving The Social Services For Those Most In Need* (Home Office Press Release, 16 July, 1969).

7 *Mental Illness in Four London Boroughs* (Psychiatric Rehabilitation Association, 1968).

8 See E. M. Goldberg and S. L. Morrison in *British Journal of Psychiatry* 109, 785 (1963).

9 *The Cost of Mental Care* (Office of Health Economics, 1965).

IAN HENDERSON

Falling Through the Net: Vagrancy

In earlier and more honestly brutal ages than our own, the various categories of the under-privileged discussed in this book were the subjects of popular jest. Physically or mentally handicapped people were objects of ridicule to their fellows. We had our 'nigger' minstrel, our comic-postcard 'queers' and, of course, the most popular of all 'them-and-us' jokes was the tramp. At the same time as William Booth's *In Darkest England*[1] was in the booksellers' windows, *Punch* scarcely let a week pass without publishing a caricature of a 'gentleman of the road', red-nosed, tattered, with his belongings wrapped in a spotted handkerchief and invariably a smile on his face.

The other, truer, side of vagrancy was one of unbelievable sordidness and horror. Jack London's vivid portraits of vagrants[2] at the turn of the century are still hard to read without a shudder of compassion. The joke tramp was always, for example, portrayed as the apotheosis of freedom. He chose the open road because its glorious liberty compensated for its discomforts. Jack London showed that even liberty of person was denied to the shivering and starving wanderer. 'Carrying the banner', as the vagrants themselves called it, meant being forced to wander the streets of London in drenching rain and murderous frosts, hounded all night long by the police whose instructions were to keep vagrants, male and female, 'on the move'. This practice and today's habit of periodically 'cleaning out' the waiting-rooms of the main railway termini by police patrols are both remnants of ancient legislation which aimed at abolishing vagrancy by terror. Jeremy Sandford states that much of the Establishment's attitude to single homeless persons can be traced back to an Act 'for the Punishment of Idle and Disorderly Persons, and

Rogues and Vagabonds', to which His Majesty King George IV
gave Royal Assent on 21 June, 1824.

The vagrants whom Booth and London met in the last years of
Victoria's reign were very much the same kind of people George
Orwell encountered while researching for *Down and Out in London
and Paris*[3] some thirty years later. The vagrant of that pre-Keynes-
ian, pre-welfare society was a tragic but explicable figure. He was a
chronic sufferer from a disease which afflicted the majority of the
population in varying degrees. The cyclical pattern of trade boom
and slump with its accompanying employment cycle was a familiar
and accepted part of life. Ironically enough, many of the finer
spirits of the times, especially Christian philanthropists such as Booth
himself, resigned themselves to accepting the industrial system as
it was. In their readiness to over-simplify the issue, they usually
looked for some Great Enemy and found it in alcohol. As they
preached total abstinence with moving fervour, they overlooked
completely the wastage and the social contradictions of the economic system. Although the system has changed out of recognition,
their attitudes are paralleled by the outlook of many social agencies
today who deal with the problems of vagrancy.

In theory, society recovered through the Laws of the Market from
recessions. In practice, thousands of the millions who had stumbled
fell, never to rise again. They were the tramps, the vagrants for
whom the trauma of unemployment had permanently shattered
any kind of settled life pattern, however mean. Most of the derelicts
described by Booth come into this category. They had all 'fallen on
hard times'. Many deceived themselves for years believing that all
they needed was a 'fair chance'. Often they belonged to seasonal or
declining trades or had once owned small businesses which had gone
bankrupt. Not infrequently, they suffered from chronic ill health.
Jack London tells how two of the inmates of a dosshouse where
he stayed had started on the downward path through contracting
smallpox. Before that, they had been in regular employment.
Finally, old age and unmarketability in a society with a permanent
labour glut, accounted for the most tragic of the drop-outs of
Victorian and Edwardian society.

The great Depression of the inter-war years may have come after
the beginnings of the Welfare State and the introduction of such
ameliorative measures as old-age pensions, but the pattern of

poverty was unchanged. The vagrant was just a very poor man among poor men, and one individual could run the entire gauntlet of poverty. A man in a depressed area who had perhaps followed a regular pattern of employment since boyhood would find himself on short-time. This would be followed by intermittent unemployment, each new job bringing him further down the ladder of security and respectability one rung at a time, the gap between each being progressively wider. Finally, he would get trapped in the rut of permanent idleness and in some instances would scrape together a few personal belongings, desert his family and take to the open road. Another recruit had joined the long marching column of homeless wanderers.

Because of the historical background of vagrancy it is not surprising that the architects of the Welfare State did not regard it as a separate problem apart from run-of-the-mill poverty. They set about tackling the root cause, the widespread poverty of the working class, with a confident and genuine expectation that the worst manifestations of poverty, the derelict and the tramp, would also fade away in the process. In 1948, the last workhouses were closed and replaced by reception centres. The purpose of the latter was to provide basic food and shelter for the single homeless person sufficient to enable him to obtain an abode and employment. The responsibility for centralized cash benefit in cases of need was vested in the newly-created National Assistance Board while indoor relief such as that afforded by the reception centres became the concern of the local authorities. At a much later date this in turn was taken out of the hands of local authorities and vested in the National Assistance Board. With the merging of the Ministry of Health with that of Social Security, reception centres became the responsibility of the Supplementary Benefits Commission of the Department of Health and Social Security. Perhaps it should be added that the care of vagrants is one of the last areas of public welfare where, despite the existence of statutory provision, there has been a willingness to leave much of the problem to be tackled by voluntary agencies. This however does not substantially alter the argument being advanced in this study. The attitudes to vagrancy which are most open to criticism in the official sector are reproduced with depressing fidelity in the voluntary field.

The expectations of those who brought the Welfare State into being were not fulfilled. Perhaps the success with which this country has abolished primary poverty among the mass of people is responsible for hiding the fact that it has not been notably successful in dealing with the vagrant. When the vagrant is noticed, he or she is curiously more strongly resented than before. The Victorian bourgeoisie accepted the beggar as a part of the landscape. Early Victorian photographs often show studies of appealing barefoot urchins taken to provoke sentimentality rather than compassion. Today, vagrants are seen only in certain twilight areas of big cities, on railway stations, hanging around the doors of churches and convents. Unconsciously, the average citizen refuses to believe they exist at all, so he falls back on rationalizations about layabouts and boozers and 'Irishmen' who prefer tramping to working. Newspapers and even Members of Parliament work themselves into a frenzy over the possibility of a few thousand people who are supposedly conning social security benefit. Strangely, these arguments in an entirely different social context are very similar to the rationalizations that our grandfathers used to enable *them* to tolerate the sight of dereliction and human decay. 'And so, dear soft people,' wrote Jack London, 'Should you ever visit London Town and see these men asleep on the benches and on the grass in Green Park, please do not think they are lazy creatures, preferring sleep to work. Know that the powers that be have kept them walking all night long, and that in the day they have nowhere else to sleep.'

That was written seventy years ago. But you can still see men sleeping on the benches of Green Park or in the main railway stations. London also wrote of 'the welter of rags and filth, of all manner of loathsome skin diseases, open sores, bruises, grossness, indecency, leering monstrosities and bestial faces' that lay all around him in Itchy Park, Spitalfields. Today the same spectacle, provided by scores of vagrant 'Jacks' or methylated spirits drinkers who use the Park as their dormitory, can be seen by the curious and the concerned. But among the mass of Londoners, curiosity or concern about vagrancy in the nineteen-seventies is depressingly rare.

How Many?

One of the most elusive social statistics is an exact identification of the number of men and women in Great Britain who at the present

F

time come within the official classification of 'homeless single persons
of no fixed abode'. The adjective 'single' does not refer to marital
status but to current way of life. There are few permanent liaisons
among vagrants, although a very large number, perhaps 80 per
cent, have at some time in their lives been married or have been
cohabiting. The psychopathology of the modern social drop-out
and the type of care that the community provides, mean that such
liaisons have long ago been severed or cannot exist for more than a
very brief period.

In 1965, the most recent of the large-scale surveys of homeless
single persons was conducted by the old National Assistance Board
helped by a number of voluntary agencies. They placed homeless
single persons in one of four categories : persons sleeping rough,
persons using reception centres, persons using lodging house and
shelter-type accommodation and, finally, persons seeking financial
help from the National Assistance Board's local offices when they
were without accommodation. The most interesting and hotly
debated figure in the Survey was that of persons sleeping rough.
This was arrived at by doing a nationwide count using NAB officials and some voluntary workers on one winter night, 6 December,
1965. The result was that 965 people, mostly men, were found 'doing
a skipper'. The Survey Report was very careful to qualify this finding by pointing out that it offered neither refutation nor confirm-
ation of estimates made previously by voluntary bodies. These
bodies quickly and publicly challenged the findings and advanced
various reasons why the official figure was so much lower than other
estimates. A social worker with a long experience of vagrants
suggested that the low figure was on account of the reluctance of
social drop-outs to allow themselves to be interrogated by investigators and quoted the case of one man who had told him that, such
was his dread of being questioned by 'authority' that he just kept
on walking all night. A Vicar of a rather down-at-heel parish in
South London discovered that no investigator had accosted the two
tramps who often slept in his church porch because the National
Assistance Board had apparently given instructions that private
property was not to be entered !

As the 1965 Survey discovered, it was hard to disentangle the
statistics of those who habitually slept rough from the men and
women using hostels and reception centres. A more recent private

estimate of 'sleepers rough' in London, quoted by Colonel Bovan, formerly Chief Secretary to the Salvation Army Men's Social Services, is 5,000, although other estimates are higher. *The Times* at the time of the national census reckoned that 10,000 men and women came into the category of 'homeless single persons' in London, while today over the whole country there are as many as 100,000. Jeremy Sandford in his introduction to the novel adapted from his TV play, *Edna, the Inebriate Woman*,[4] also quoted 100,000 as the figure for the whole country.

An authoritative figure was quoted by Sir Keith Joseph in May 1972. In announcing his plans for the extension of local authority social services, the Secretary of State for Social Services posed a typical community of about a quarter of a million inhabitants. In such a community could be found 100 or so 'drifters and vagrants including a few drug addicts'. On this basis, we could arrive at a national figure of 20,000 single homeless persons.

The cardinal error in calculating such numbers is to believe that sleeping rough, hostel living, and lodging house usage are separate and static ways of life. Nearly all the drifting population of homeless single persons vary their habits according to season, finance and temperament. Several women sleeping on Waterloo Station (where up to 100 people have been found sleeping rough on any one night) stated that they frequently did casual jobs—washing-up in restaurants and hotels is a common choice—and were just able to afford five nights in lodging houses, leaving two nights when they would be forced to 'skipper'. The closure of many large lodging houses and the decision of Rowton Hotels to move their interests from hostels to more profitable hotels has made the situation of these people more difficult.

The Anatomy of a Vagrant

Today's vagrant is not a grubby reminder of an old and persistent problem but a more frightening witness to a new one. He or she is not a hangover from pre-Welfare, pre-affluent Britain whose existence will soon be abolished by greater doses of affluence and Welfare. The modern vagrant is, I contend, a new creation, the rotten fruit of the kind of society which we have been busily and proudly creating for the past quarter of a century. The American theologian, Harvey Cox, celebrated the advent of the 'technopolis' as a liberation of the human spirit, while Western politicians have vied with each other (until recently) to proclaim the universal benefit of urban industrial society in a technological age. Christopher Booker[5] in his perceptive history of the 1950s and 1960s shows that as a nation we were captivated by a neophiliac fantasy. Harold Wilson transformed the Labour Party and won the 1964 General Election not by a vision of an egalitarian or even a fraternal society but by the promise of a 'dynamic' one, a society in which the computer was a god and the vesture of its votaries the white coat of the laboratory technician. Ten years ago terms like 'alienation' were part of the esoteric vocabulary of neo-Marxists and a small coterie of sociologists with an interest in psycho-analysis. Today, the environmental crisis has brought about a public reaction which is beginning to see technology and urbanization as dispensers of as many threats as benefits. An example of this new awareness can be seen in this extract from the celebrated and controversial issue of *The Ecologist* in the autumn of 1971, 'A Blueprint for Survival' :

> There is every reason to believe that the social ills at present afflicting our society—increasing crime, delinquency, vandalism, alcoholism as well as drug addiction—are closely related and are the symptoms of the breakdown of our cultural pattern which in turn is an aspect of the disintegration of our society. These tendencies can only be accentuated by further demographic and economic growth. It is chimeric to suppose that any of these tendencies can be checked by the application of external controls or by treating them in isolation, i.e. apart from the social disease of which they are but symptoms.

The vagrant is a chronic symptom of that social disease just as the tramp in Victorian England was a chronic symptom of widespread working-class poverty. One feature of modern urban society is its fragmentation, leading to the condition that David Reisman called 'The Lonely Crowd'. The other is the complexity of the decision-making process. In a primary society, the number of decisions and choices are limited. In the technopolis they are manifold. The increasing use of numerical data has its confusing side. The intro-duction of all-figure telephone numbers caused one psychologist to comment that the human memory is normally capable of remember-

ing only six digits at a time. Nowhere is this aspect of life so promin-
ent as in the complex apparatus of Welfare; yet ironically those
who are least intellectually equipped to cope with such complications
have most need to tackle them, for the poor and underprivileged
are dependent on Welfare. They have no accountants and advisers
to manage their financial affairs which, strange as it may seem to the
average middle-range executive, are in their context as complicated
as his.

The confrontation with choice and decision-making is most terri-
fying at the lowest end of the scale. In order to obtain a bed in a
hostel or reception centre, more decisions have to be made. The
admittee has either to find the money to pay or (in the case of
reception centres and some voluntary hostels) he or she has to offer
proof of destitution. Both can be equally traumatic. If the individual
in question does gain admission to a reception centre run by the
Department of Health and Social Security, he is then compelled to
answer a questionnaire about work, habitation, place of birth,
criminal or clinical record and marital status. Refusal to answer
can lead to summary dismissal. If however he manages to cope with
the sheer mechanics of admission, he still faces a crash course in
dehumanization. He is stripped and his clothes and body searched
for lice with the aid of a portable inspection light such as car
mechanics use for close work on an internal combustion engine. His
clothes are then put in a patent plastic bag and de-infested by a
baking process. This is extremely damaging to cloth, and there are
frequent bitter complaints when the shapeless and ruined suit or
dress is reclaimed. Too often it was the only decent article of clothing the inmate possessed. Despite the spirited common-sense arguments which reception centre staff advance to justify these admission rituals, the result, intentional or not, is to strip an individual
of the last vestiges of self-respect.

Many urban vagrants come from the Celtic fringes of our society,
which fact has led some commentators to suggest that their problems
are primarily economic and the socio-psychological argument advanced here without foundation. A little light on the psychology of
immigration and migration is necessary. As a general rule all
migrants fall into two categories: those who are more intelligent
and socially proficient than the norms of their mother culture, and
those who are less so. This is not to suggest that only representatives

of these extremes migrate or emigrate, but it is true to say that they are the first to leave. The ambitious Scotsman or Irishman or Welshman who arrives in the big city is too well known to need description. The migration of the weaker, less able elements is not so well understood. Their reason is partly economic—work is scarce and wages low—but also psycho-social. If work is going, they are least likely to be offered it. If wages increase in one area, they are not among the beneficiaries. In short, it is the potential drop-out (the educationally sub-normal, the inadequate, the border-line schizophrenic) who migrates to the big cities and quickly falls through the safety net into drink, drugs, petty crime and general rootlessness.

In a primary society, despite the lack of economic advantages, the mentally immature are accorded a place, however lowly. The village idiot was very often little more than a vagrant but he was recognized as having a right to exist. He was aware of himself as a person. This kind of containment process is totally missing from modern urban society and has only occasionally been reproduced in the environment of a few experimental hostels.

Patterns of Behaviour

One of the most unfortunate exaggerations of the problem of modern vagrancy is the suggestion which is made explicitly in the popular press that all vagrants are alcoholics and even crude spirit-drinkers. The horrifyingly bizarre characteristics of the 'meths man' are obvious material for descriptive journalism. Although alcoholics in steady manual and clerical employment occasionally end up on Skid Row, this is not a typical behaviour pattern. Timothy Cook[6] has estimated that the vagrant alcoholic represents only 5 per cent of the total alcoholic population, although the incidence of alcoholism among homeless single persons has been judged by some to be as high as 45 per cent. In an investigation which formed part of the National Assistance Board survey already mentioned, 838 men from the reception centres were subjected to medical examination, and 28 per cent were found to be dependent on alcohol or had a chronic drinking problem. In the same year, Dr Griffith Edwards and three clinical colleagues from the Institute of Psychiatry at the Maudsley Hospital found that of 279 men in the London Men's

Reception Centre at Camberwell, 25 per cent were chemically dependent upon alcohol and another 20 per cent showed signs of an acute drinking problem.

These and other clinical surveys show the high incidence of mental illness among homeless single persons. Of those investigated in the NAB survey, 26 per cent were mentally ill. In 1970,[7] based admittedly on a smaller sample of 122 men who used lodging houses, Dr Lodge-Patch found that 15 per cent were schizophrenic, 10 per cent mentally sub-normal and 50 per cent suffering from a personality disorder. The incidence of mental illness is also matched by physical illness so that half those interviewed suffered some form of severe or moderate physical disability.

The fact that emergency hostel-type accommodation has become a substitute for psychiatric after-care is too notorious to need stressing. The Women's Reception Centre in Southwark some years ago agreed that its intake was similar to that of a well-known voluntary hostel operating only a mile away. The Wardens of both establishments suggested that 70 per cent of the women admitted each night were mentally ill and in need of treatment. The inability of National Health psychiatry to cope successfully with personality disorders means that many hospitals are only too eager to discharge a patient if a hostel or reception centre can accommodate him.

Some workers in the vagrancy field would claim that social inadequacy is a new illness pattern, sometimes but not inevitably associated with other forms of mental illness. Anton Wallich-Clifford describes social inadequacy as 'the inability to face up to demands, responsibilities and pressures of life within the normal framework of society', and adds that social inadequacy is recognized as a 'disease entity' in Scandinavia, recommending legislation of a similar kind in Britain.[8] Certainly, as Jeremy Sandford has suggested, the first step towards a more humane and therapeutic approach to the care and treatment of social deviants is a drastic revision of the laws governing our attitudes to vagrancy.

There is a great deal of truth in David Brandon's suggestion that harsh treatment of vagrants has historical and cultural associations with a Protestant ethical tradition.[9] Coupled with a belief in salvation through work and self-reliance, this tradition finds no place for the holy man, the itinerant mystic, the recluse. Even the arts are regarded as an aspect of industry. The doctrine of the sanctity of work has outlived the heyday of its religious inspiration but still largely governs our attitude to the care and treatment of vagrancy. It prevents a general acceptance that some vagrants are permanently unsuited to life in competitive society, and over-emphasizes treatment aimed at putting the individual back into the production line. In this respect the approach pioneered by Anton Wallich-Clifford and the Simon Community deserves special con-sideration because of its originality. It is unfortunate that schisms within the original Simon Community coupled with financial prob-lems have prevented Wallich-Clifford from realizing some of his more ambitious projects, but they nevertheless deserve an honour-able mention even if they are unlikely to materialize in the im-mediate future.

Wallich-Clifford, a former London probation officer and a devout Roman Catholic who was once studying for the priesthood, laid the foundations of Simon in the early 1960s. Its main philosophical inspiration was a belief in the essential humanity of the vagrant and a willingness to see Christ in even the most abandoned character. Simon workers, who often included former 'dossers', identified with the vagrant by taking quasi-Franciscan vows of poverty ('a quid a week pocket money, a tobacco allowance and a wardrobe of hand-outs') and living on equal terms within Simon Houses of Hospitality with those who were being cared for. 'Simon', writes Wallich-Clifford in his book *The Simon Scene*, 'does not seek to rehabilitate but to *contain*. Its aim is to accept, assimilate and then sort out. By the passing on of those who have responded and indicated their ability to graduate, and by the containment in a state of non-offending self-help of those who require permanent membership, it may be judged to have "rehabilitated" its residents. Simon workers, however, should not fall into the trap of aiming to restore to an unsympathetic society the men and women who, over and over again, have failed most, if not all, formal attempts to cure them.'

Not the least important strand of Wallich-Clifford's thinking is that the society with which the vagrant is at odds is itself wrong and that there can be no satisfactory solution to the vagrancy prob-lem while society is governed by what Erich Fromm calls 'the marketing ethos' and human beings are judged for the most part by their market value.[10]

Towards an Answer

A final answer to the problem of vagrancy today is not possible within the framework of our present society but there are a number of useful indicators mostly based upon experimentation with care techniques by such bodies as the Simon Community and Christian Action. It is unlikely that voluntary societies, however, will be able to take care of all those needing care and containment without massive subsidization from public funds. Perhaps this would be the most imaginative way of tackling the problem. It is however much more likely that the voluntary units will continue to be regarded by the Department of Health and Social Security as experimental units and that, while subsidization on a more modest scale may be extended, the best that can be hoped for is that the experiments will inspire re-organization of reception centres and local authority provision for homeless single persons.

The first need in this process of reshaping statutory accommodation is a large-scale de-centralization of the existing units. Reception centres serving one metropolis like that at present run by the Department of Health and Social Security in Camberwell simply defy the most talented clinical techniques. On the basis of experience among the newer and more original voluntary organizations, units of not more than twenty have been found to be most effective.

The second requirement for a therapeutic environment is the relaxation of admission rituals and even standards of cleanliness. Most of the successful voluntary enterprises function from choice in old, rather dilapidated houses, where the atmosphere of a hostel or institution gives way to the atmosphere of a home in the real sense of the word. Similarly, the rule that stipulates that the individual seeking help must be subjected to compulsory cleansing and disinfection, to a bombardment of questions and even form-filling must be relaxed. In practice the voluntary units find, with smaller number of admissions and higher standards of training among the staff of the units, that quite tolerable standards of hygiene can be maintained.

This brings us to a third stipulation : that the staff of all units for

the care and treatment of single homeless people must be trained to
perform a therapeutic task. Shortage of social workers and inadequate salaries mean that most reception centre staff (who perform an arduous and thankless task) are not trained for the job.
Nor do the units usually include more than one or two medical
officers and even then not necessarily those with psychiatric training and experience. Social workers who are concerned with the care
and treatment of social drop-outs ought to undergo a complete
Psychiatric Social Worker's course and be given regular supportive
aid through group therapy. Ideally, they ought in time to be capable
of organizing group work themselves among their charges. It is a
legitimate criticism that until very recent years the emphasis in this
kind of social work has been on social 'admin.' rather than on
therapeutic skills.

Fourthly, coupled with an overhaul of existing provision for
homeless single persons, there is a desperate need for the expansion
of psychiatric after-care facilities which would in so many cases
provide a therapeutic alternative to reception centre and shelter
accommodation. A former Secretary of State for the Social Services
when taken by the author on a tour of reception centres and voluntary units in South London was shocked to discover the high
incidence of mental illness and incipient mental disorder among
men and women using this kind of accommodation. Psychiatric
after-care is one of the cinderellas of the Welfare State. Adequate
provision of facilities would be costly but any improvement in this
field would inevitably involve extra cost. It is, like every other aspect
of an anti-poverty programme, a matter of priorities.

Fifthly and finally, there is a need to face up to the problem of
untreatable social nonconformity, something which Wallich-Clifford
was among the first to realize. Basing his suggestions on experiments with recidivists and vagrant alcoholics, he proposed the
idea of self-supporting village communities which would reflect the
controlled permissiveness of Simon Houses of Hospitality as a permanent way of life. This kind of project involves a large outlay and
is almost certainly beyond the scope of voluntary enterprise. The
important lesson to be learned from this proposal is our readiness
to accept as part of society some men and women who are in-
capable of being reclaimed for regular, ordered existence as we
understand it. The problem of recidivism is very much bound up

with this fact. The late Fr George Potter, an Anglican Franciscan well-known in the years between the wars for his work among prisoners, visited a hardened criminal in Dartmoor. 'Well,' said Fr George, 'You're here again. You must like it here!' The reply was significant. 'Well, Father, it's funny you should say that. The only places I feel at home in are behind bars or in your Friary.' For some people an enclosed life, replacing the virtually non-existent community of society at large, is a necessity if they are to survive.

A final question the reader might well ask is this: why should society be prepared to give such painstaking attention to the problems of a tiny minority who, so far from being grateful, may even respond by literally biting the helping hand? I find it impossible to produce any satisfactory humanistic answer. My own philosophy of care is rooted in the Christian faith and can only be explained in the context of that faith. I believe that if Christianity has anything to teach the world it is that after all the good, secular, compassionate reasons for caring have been exhausted, when on grounds of social prudence nothing more can be done for a man, the Christian must carry on regardless. God never gives up—not even the most abandoned blackguard imaginable. His followers have no choice but to carry on loving; loving and forgiving until seven times seventy, which is just another way of expressing infinity.

NOTES

1 William Booth, *In Darkest England and A Way Out* (Salvationist Publishing & Supplies Ltd, 1890).

2 Jack London, *People of the Abyss* (Isbister, 1903).

3 George Orwell, *Down and Out in London and Paris* (Gollancz, 1933).

4 Jeremy Sandford, *Edna, The Inebriate Woman* (Pan Books, 1971).

5 Christopher Booker, *The Neophiliacs* (Collins, 1969).

6 Timothy Cook, 'The Vagrant Alcoholic: A Social Problem', *Update*, 1 January, 1972.

7 I. C. Lodge-Patch, *Proceedings of the Royal Society of Medicine* (1970), p. 63.

8 Anton Wallich-Clifford, *The Simon Scene* (Housman, 1968).

9 David Brandon, *Homeless In London* (Christian Action, 1971).

10 Erich Fromm, *The Sane Society* (Routledge & Kegan Paul, 1956).

WATSON JENKINS

Reviewing Retirement

He sat in a corner of the room, his long, white beard almost to his knees as he hunched in his chair. His thin hand stroked his brow. He did not speak and did not seem to care for the meeting, which went on without reference to him. But as we left the room, we repeated the respects we had paid him on entering : with us were an American congressman, a bishop, a rabbi and others with names of distinction from homes thousands of miles away, together with leading members of the Saigon Bar. The old Vietnamese may have had little in common with his son's guests, but they all respected him for his age.

In Britain, by contrast, old age automatically confers on most people a second-rate citizenship. While retirement can bring real practical problems with it, the primary hardship is that an old person is not afforded the social standing he enjoys in many other countries. Even in Europe, although nothing can compare with the deferential treatment given by many Asian societies to the oldest members of the family, there are still places where the social climate is kinder to the old.

Emancipation from the dominance of the old in family life has been steadily growing over the last hundred years. In the affluent West the process is complete. Affluence itself, the mobility of society and changing morality have all contributed to the breakdown of old patterns. In Britain the days of arranged marriages and young men who called their fathers 'Sir' are largely past. Only among the new immigrant families can the iron rule of the *paterfamilias* still be observed.

168

Any review of the conditions of retirement will inevitably find sad evidence of the slowing down of communication between the generations, both within the family group and outside it. There is increasing breakdown of family relationships and of the family itself as a social unit. Housing conditions have changed. We live in flats, or in houses half the size of those in which our grandparents were brought up. This reduction in space has deprived spinster aunts, elderly parents or other weaker members of the family of a natural place to live. It is not only because of the willingness of the State to care for those on the fringes of medical need that we pack the elderly off to hospitals and Homes : the conditions in which we live are considerably more cramped than they once were.

Grandmothers and grandfathers, great uncles and great aunts are not the force they used to be in the family circle. Children now grow up in an atmosphere of diminished responsibility and contact. In a sense, too, family life is not as caring as it used to be, and children quickly learn from their parents that the problems of retirement belong to the retired. In fact, although Grandma may have strong and not always welcome ideas on the religious, sexual and financial standards of the family, her usefulness in complementing the role of the parents can be of great value. Once the younger family has severed contact—by personal attitudes or by the fact of removal to a distance where real contact is difficult—the life-giving element in the relationship is largely at an end.

By the multiplicity of family relationships thus destroyed, society has dealt itself a body blow, but in no way more destructive than among the members of the older generation. Those who have retired now find their most congenial companions in their own age-group. Only a few maintain a place among the young, by involvement in currently fashionable enterprises or by their sheer inability to wither at the usual speed. For the rest there is a greater sense of social decline than the old have ever felt before. This is despite the safeguards to health which have prolonged active life, for inactive life has also been prolonged. Once it was rare to reach seventy; now octogenarians are commonplace. Today it is quite common for people to spend twenty years in social frailty, frequently tucked away from the mainstream of family life and active participation in society, in Homes and hospital wards.

The real issue is the broad one of how society is going to tackle the progressive imbalance between the young and the old, and whether we can do something to make sure that action on a national scale is forthcoming.

The housing situation faced by the retired is the best-known aspect of the problem of retirement. The whole question of how and when retirement comes, although a separate issue, should be linked to any discussion of housing and financial need. The way in which workers are discharged from employment raises both the industrial issue of how a person may keep pace with changing working conditions and industrial needs, and the more personal issue of how he may face changes in society as a whole.

The ties older people have with family and friends are conducive both to health and happiness; so also is the moral and political role which they exercise in the community. They have suffered a loss of morale; their personal dignity has been attacked, if not fatally undermined. Therefore, most of our elderly citizens would find it reassuring to know that strong social policies were being envisaged which would effectively reduce this painful sense of inferiority and uselessness. It is essential to restore the sense of self-respect that will come from knowing they can still play some part in the society they have helped to build.

Man is not an island. He depends upon others, as others depend upon him. Childhood, youth, prime of life and old age succeed each other at an inexorable pace, in a cycle no one can halt. We cannot choose the manner in which we come into the world; with luck and compassionate foresight, we can control the manner in which we leave it.

Housing in Retirement

In the old days many people never retired; if they did it was in order that they might live on in the family home and within the family circle until they died. But now the plight of the few has become the lot of the many. Stricter rules concerning the retirement of workers, aided by the provision of the State pension, have ruled out the prospect of working until one drops. Better medical care has ensured a life prolonged past retirement age, but inflation and insufficient family help have in many cases shattered the hope of remaining on in the old home with the family, or even of living near them.

At first sight one might expect that the problem of housing would be most acute among the working class. Extremes of poverty are normally most readily found among unskilled workers. But society does not produce easy divisions in this respect. The fact that the middle class may have savings does not necessarily make it prosperous, for the effect of inflation on savings and continuing escalation in the cost of property can lead to very real hardship as time goes on. There is often just as much worry about the management of affairs in Acacia Avenue as in Coronation Street. Superannuation and annuity policies which supplement the pension may lessen the difficulty for many of the middle class. But the widow who survives after superannuation ceases, burdened by a larger, colder and more expensive house than her working-class counterpart, is not necessarily in a happier state, unless instinct combines with common sense and she sells out and finds a flat instead.

In this respect, men and women who have been brought up in comfortable circumstances suffer far more. To 'come down in the world' has always been a very real fear with the middle-class worker who has tried all his life to 'keep respectable' and 'hold up his head' among his neighbours. The Victorian music-hall song has a very potent chorus :

> Too proud to beg, too honest to steal,
> I know what it is to be wanting a meal.
> My tatters and rags I try to conceal . . .
> Oh, what it is to be shabby genteel !

Pride will often make a widow struggle on in cruelly reduced circumstances because any financial help from outside the family carries with it the terrible stigma of charity. Thanks to a growing acceptance of Social Security as a right rather than a hateful handout, this attitude is changing. But pride also makes for loneliness, another factor of old age which is even less bearable than poverty.

The most casual investigation also reveals the fact that many old people are troubled in the extreme about money and budgeting for their various needs. The cost of living is a burden often much greater than was the burden of work, or of bringing up a family.

The old survive mainly because their demands are less urgent, but in too many cases the word 'survive' is all too appropriate.

In addition to the cost of housing, which by means of supplementary benefits can be regularized after a fashion, there is the problem of the type of housing in which the retired live. Many cannot afford a house or flat and resort to living in a single room. In many cases the upkeep of the house or room is the responsibility of the landlord, not the old person himself. Social workers and ministers are told of the iniquities of landlords. Although right is often on the side of the old person who complains, there is no doubt that landlords of some controlled tenancies also find themselves in a difficult situation. Indeed, it is this very financial difficulty which is progressively leading to the destruction of low-cost accommodation with minimal controlled rents. As a result, there are progressively fewer economical homes and flats for retired people to rent, alongside the ever-increasing demand for them. Many old people who are unhappy living alone, or who feel victimized, do not relish the thought of going into a Home. Private Homes are above their means, and places in State-run Homes are either difficult to find or leave much to be desired in the way of amenities.

In a complex and difficult situation, voluntary schemes, housing associations and local authority enterprise nibble away at the problem. The basic situation is left untouched and is growing in size. However much the government of the day raises the retirement pension, it does not seem that the problem of housing will be overcome. Pensions barely keep pace with basic costs and in a country with a constant pressure on housing, an increased cash payment will not readily solve the problem of how to ensure fair distribution.

The difficulties are twofold : how best to help those who can no longer live independently, and how to produce a workable social scheme which will allow and encourage active retired people to live independently in the neighbourhood of their choice and not in isolated conditions.

Too often the old are moved away from their homes and familiar surroundings where friends are a support to them, to unfamiliar, impersonal places. These may be more 'suitable' in terms of room heating and size and age of accommodation. But any action which deprives elderly men and women of friends at a time when making friends is difficult, and pulls up their roots when they are most needed deprives them of a different kind of warmth. No wonder that on hundreds of slum clearance estates the same social problem arises : how to persuade the old to move out. The shape of the hills and the contours of the roads, the familiar smell of the corner shop and the feel of the sixth pew on the right hand side at Bethel *are* life for them. Anything that destroys these things destroys what has been true living for maybe more than half a century. The old almhouses, despite their recent public image of being decayed and inadequate relics of outdated charity, had the great advantage of providing for people in their own parish. Their renewal and re-placement in some areas is proving a successful approach to this problem which could well be copied.

Just as national pension and supplementary benefits, the free health service and free education sprang from provision for the poor made by the Church in the first instance, so today we have a further opportunity. This is to build on the foundation of the almshouses and discover a new principle for our welfare society. Those who are old need the full protection of society and due reward for their labours. *The State should provide the retired with universal free accommodation.* This should be the object of our present efforts for housing in old age.

How much we should ask the worker to contribute out of his income towards State Welfare provisions is hard to assess. Whether the provision of free accommodation on retirement should be financed by charges levied directly on the worker or indirectly through, for example, a land tax, is not an issue for this chapter. It must be noted, however, that the present retirement pension is already closely associated with the provision of accommodation. This is one of the main problems for the State to face. It might be possible to make a realistic assessment of the cost of housing in a society where most old people were housed in nationally-owned property, but this is not our present situation. Housing costs are subject to all the excesses of our inflationary capitalist system. The rents paid by the retired directly assist the profits of property com-panies. Thus the pension provisions of the many, paid through the retired to property owners, become the profit margins of the few. What must be accepted is that this is not only wasteful but in-herently wrong, if the nation is to provide universal free accom-modation for the old.

In tackling a great social reform the overriding difficulty is that of making a real impression on the existing situation. The first stage of a free accommodation policy will inevitably be some alternative form of grant aid. If the retirement pension as such did not carry with it the burden of housing provision, it could be reduced initially and a housing grant given separately. This grant might itself have strings attached so as to give the State an opportunity of coming into the worst housing situations and effecting improvements. Moreover, such conditions should be tackled much more insistently than they are at present. Many of the old living in rotting premises and overcrowded slums have for too long been dependent upon the good offices of voluntary workers to improve their property.

Free retirement accommodation should be available to everyone, whether they are living with their children or in their own house, in a hotel or an old people's Home. An upper limit on help would preclude the affluent who may prefer to live in a baronial mansion. But there could be real incentives, matched by some degree of compulsion, for local authorities and voluntary societies to provide accommodation of a high standard.

We do not want everyone to live in some form of retirement ghetto. This is a present danger for those who are locked away in larger local authority Homes or who occupy beds in geriatric hospitals. In many areas the simple provisions of a Meals-on-Wheels service, a home help or a visiting nurse, a voluntary or church worker, are fairly adequate and will do while general standards are being raised. The real opportunity however is seen to have been taken up in isolated experiments like the complex in Amsterdam where a central hospital unit is surrounded by homes for both families and the retired to live in close proximity to one another. We need to be saved from the seaside town disease of emasculated society where the old live in bungalows and the young get out as soon as they can. Even an almshouse is too often clearly identified as a place for the indigent old. A better idea would be the provision of special blocks of flats interspersed in new housing developments as a compulsory norm, in the same way that hospitals and some well-run industries take as workers their complement of the disabled.

There is no doubt that housing schemes, with or without resident wardens and helpers, are not and never can be a true substitute for a society that cares. The Church and a large number of voluntary bodies can attempt to fill needs to some extent, but our real objective should be the re-establishment of care by the family. Making it possible for families to want to stay together is crucial and deserves our special attention.

Old people with no income apart from their retirement pension are by no means the only ones to suffer unnecessarily from a separation from their families. Old people with small personal incomes are often among the first to find themselves moved away from their middle-aged children, who do not feel obliged to provide a home for their partly-independent parents. As long as grandchildren are young, the problem of accommodating grandparents in the same small house is not insoluble. It is when the grandchildren become teenagers, needing more living space, that the situation may become difficult. Teenage boys and girls must have separate bedrooms, for example, and this may not leave one for Grandma. A few years later, when the children have left home, parents can more readily accommodate the grandparents, but by this time vital decisions may have been taken : a Home has been found for the old person to go to, or else the old person, having inured herself to new routines, is unwilling to make another change.

How can we make it possible for families to live together at times of maximum pressure on the living space available? The answer is not necessarily to exchange the house for a bigger one. A maisonette, a couple of streets away, converted by the local authority or a housing association for the provision of free accommodation, may help to meet the problem. The 'swopping' facilities already exploited by councils with council housing could be utilized. Planning permission could be obtained, together with full improvement grants, for the provision of a controlled 'retirement flat' in certain properties.

For those retired people who own their property and whose main difficulty is meeting the rising costs of upkeep, on fixed incomes, there is a further step to be taken. This is to make the property itself subject to an equitable interest by the State, redeemable only on sale or on the death of the occupant. In this way also the State may usefully intervene to help, giving the advice on housing repairs and proper maintenance that so many need.

There are many variations on such a theme, including the revision of our attitudes to old people's Homes, and the service given by hospitals. Within the bounds of reason, the State should make the accommodation of the retired everywhere free of charge. People should have in retirement the security of a permanent home, worthy of the name. There must be general freedom of choice, but the weakest should have special protection through the personal assistance of State officers. Old people can be encouraged to vacate places too big or too expensive for them, not by coercion but by the provision of something obviously better for them and for their long-term welfare. There can be no reform more pressing than to give retired people a new deal in housing.

Work in Retirement

In Britain the pressure on people to work is very mild, compared with that in communist countries. In effective terms, the highest standards of living come to the society that makes the most intensive use of its labour, coupled with a high degree of technology. Britain is moving only slowly towards such a position. In the fields of industrial training, the mobility of labour, the employment of women and the full use of the retired there is a long way to go.

The employment of the retired is of little significance in the present British industrial scene. There are, of course, a good number of pensioners taking on retirement jobs. At one time traffic wardens were recruited from older workers, some of whom had retired from career employment, but this job has itself now developed a career structure and a more youthful image. Even though school traffic wardens, part-time gardeners, odd-job men, cleaners and office messengers may be recruited on a basis irrespective of age, it is certain that the number of firms who will employ retired workers is strictly limited.

Many of the jobs in the community for which older workers are suited, because hours are shorter and the effort required is less, are in themselves non-productive. That is not to say that the work done is not useful, even essential, but that it does not contribute to the total manufacturing output of the country. Yet those responsible for employment do not seem to have realized that the encouragement of the retired into such work would effectively release more able-bodied workers for the manufacturing industries. At times of high unemployment it may appear illogical to give jobs to people whose normal working life is over. However, the answer to unemployment is not to be found in a reduction of the total labour force available but in the more effective use of the whole labour force, actual and potential.

There are large numbers of retired people who do not want to go on working. Some sixty-year-olds are not well enough to carry on. Many have waited a life-time for the opportunity retirement affords them to follow their own interests, unhampered by the nine-to-five slog. Such workers are in the same category as those who prefer to live where they choose and do not seek accommodation from the State. They have support from the State through the retirement pension, to which they have contributed and which is theirs by right.

But in a good many instances retirement is a personal disaster for the worker. The cessation of good wages, the abrupt ending of habitual and absorbing tasks is sometimes enough to kill a man, and often leaves him robbed of a sense of purpose and usefulness. It is not unreasonable that old age should reduce the demand for his services; the retiring generation must face the fact of age, just as the infant faces compulsory schooling and the adolescent faces the end of dependence on the family. But work means life for many people. And those who pass the magic birthday that heralds retirement do not automatically lose their capacity for work.

While there is often a great deal to be gained by continuing to use the skills of older workers, in many industries their presence is seen by others as an effective block to advancement. Young men want to get on, and the continued presence of their seniors can be a real difficulty to them. There is a case to be made for the regrouping of industrial jobs to allow workers of fifty years or more to opt for a job which does not bring with it inevitable retirement, but which gives relief from pressures that can build up dangerously after the age of fifty. The kind of work traffic wardens do is a good example and should be a symbol of the potential within industry and commerce generally. It may be that a new development in trade unionism is needed : jobs suited to retired or disabled workers could be given a special union grouping in order to make employers aware of their availability.

If we are to acknowledge that work should not necessarily cease for people at the traditional ages of retirement, then we need to express our understanding in terms of a general principle. *Pensioned workers should be encouraged to do work for which they are suited, and enjoy the benefits of that work to the full.* It is important that work done during pensionable age should not affect the giving of the State pension. It is equally important to see that industry does not take advantage of the State provision to create a 'sweat-shop' among pensioned workers. Dismissal procedures, government training schemes, medical care and many smaller issues will need thorough and creative thinking in government departments and union headquarters alike.

In the field of preventive medicine the employment of pensioners would open up new opportunities. If a fitness test were to be made obligatory before employment, this would ensure improved opportunities for pensioners and at the same time strengthen contact with social workers. Annual certificates might be awarded after some inquiry into the socio-medical situation of the worker.

The State should also seek to provide some of the employment for pensioner-workers by way of light assembly workshops, where attendance could be on a voluntary basis. Centres for Further Work, similar in organization to those for Further Education, would meet a need for many who are looking not for full-time employment but for something to supplement the pension.

There is no doubt that a great desire for further employment exists among older citizens. They should be encouraged to do what is good both for them and for the community as a whole. As Hugh Faulkner, Hon. Director of Help the Aged, wrote in a letter to *The Times* (5 December, 1972): 'It is important that independence and activity are recognized as the greatest preventers of old age.'

The Substitute Family

It is not necessary to labour the point that the family unit, formerly a great feature of British life, has become diminished in strength and effectiveness. The fact that some currently popular moral issues are involved does not make this decline easier to discuss. But however moralists may seek to reverse trends, there is reason to doubt whether the main causes of the decline lie within the realms of ethical judgement. Economic pressures, overpopulation, the difficulties of living in urban societies—all these encourage the family to become smaller and more mobile. It is hard to visualize a reversal in these trends for a long time to come.

Smaller families mean fewer relatives. Mobility brings with it a difficulty in caring for the aged members of the family. There is less contact and less time. Although the telephone can be a substitute for the 'duty' letter, it often proves not to serve the purpose, since those in telephone contact with their parents may assume that, because easy communication is possible, frequent personal contact is unnecessary.

There is a clear case for the retired, whether married or single, to find a substitute for the family. In some respects the twentieth century has provided substitutes, but we still have a long way to go. In the case of mental stimulus, the retired have never had it so good. The radio is regarded as a 'great friend', as is television. There are many programmes which cater specifically for the retired, covering interests from gardening to religion. Naturally, fading eyesight and loss of hearing render the communications media less effective, but this was always so.

Where companionship is concerned, however, the retired are not universally better off. Darby and Joan clubs are for the 'clubbable' and are resisted by a very large number, partly perhaps because of the patronizing attitudes taken by some club leaders. Many retired people do not wish to accept any such organized help and resent the feeling of helplessness which such offers create. Some of the most successful associations for the retired are those where the prime object is not to relieve boredom and loneliness but to promote some sport or activity. These could be encouraged still further by the additional help of local authority grants, for one constant drawback of all clubs is the demand for money which pensioners find quite impossible to meet at times. In the past, the Church provided a well-balanced social group of young and old; today, in many areas, it is only the retired who give any active support to local congregations. Whether the Church will eventually abandon its insistence on using local church buildings and favour house meetings instead is to be seen. The germ of the idea is there and has formed the basis for experiments, but so far the house-centred group has not been taken up locally with much enthusiasm.

Voluntary bodies need not be the only organizations to cater for the needs of the retired. Commercial interests have developed many markets, from the pre-school child to the adolescent; there is no reason why the particular interests and needs of the old should not be exploited commercially in the same way. In a predominantly commercial society, publicity which would popularize the idea of retirement as a desirable state of being might help marginally to give the old the additional status that they need.

The Final Retirement

Death is the end of retirement. For some, the thought of death is linked with the end of working life, but most of us know better. In Britain the subject of death is largely taboo, a fact that is visibly linked with the decline of belief in a religion which speaks of eternal life. While old people may be neither unaware nor unafraid of death, there are few to assist them in their anxieties.

While many aspects connected with the approach of death remain veiled, one in particular has gained in prominence. Advances in medical techniques have greatly accelerated a social problem—geriatric nursing today raises the issue of euthanasia as never before. It is now not uncommon to hear long and sad stories of aged relatives spending many months, even years, in huge wards for helpless and senile patients, or to be told in confidence how the processes of death were assisted by relatives who responded to the demand of 'let me die'. When a person is senile, schemes for housing, work or recreation become irrelevant. Old men and women lying frustrated and incontinent in rows of beds with cot sides, looked after by staff who are frequently inadequately trained and grossly overworked, are subjected to a medical technology of an advanced kind which has not been able to gear itself to social thinking.

The real issue in this situation cannot be euthanasia. The inevitable tension this issue raises is hard for those involved, but in essence it is not unlike that created by other great social problems when they are focused on the individual. Since society has not yet chosen euthanasia, and since, clearly, it is not seen as the best way out for most people, the real problem is the personal attention given to the geriatric patient. No one who has spent hours in hospital among the old can avoid coming to the conclusion that our methods of approach to geriatric nursing are as old-fashioned as the padded-cell approach to the mentally ill. The one great sense which over-powers the old as they enter the geriatric ward is summed up in the line, 'Abandon hope all ye who enter here'.

Unless we do something about our geriatric wards we cannot resolve the tension and the fear of death. The last resting place of the living on earth should possess a quality of beauty and re-assurance helpful both to the patients and to those who work among them. It should be a pleasant and cheerful place, too, for friends and relatives, and an encouragement for regular visiting. As many visitors may be elderly and have no private transport, travelling facilities in the way of ambulances might well be made available to them as well as to the sick. Naturally these improvements will cost money, but when we weigh the cost against the millions squandered on supersonic aircraft and Polaris submarines, we have to regard the issue as a moral one. There is nothing so conducive to senility as the kind of indifference and neglect that sends sensitive old people out of their minds. This is happening quietly every day in this country.

There are practical remedies which could assist social progress. The cost of keeping long-term patients is heavy both upon the State and upon supporting families when these are responsible for nursing. A more determined national policy might well achieve two goals : to draw up a register of families caring for a permanent invalid, and to make dependency grants available to encourage the family to carry the burden. Home is nearly always the best place for an old person. The less sophisticated treatment may, in practice, be less conducive to long life, but it is the *quality* of life that matters. The greater availability of grants to families in those cases where the situation is difficult but not impossible, would also alleviate over-crowded conditions in hospitals.

Another innovation might well be considered. In cases where an old person has to be cared for in hospital, and where his or her income or capital reserves are sufficient, it should become standard practice to attach an order of court to the benefit of the hospital. Naturally in cases of such attachment there would have to be a standard of care to which the hospital must conform. The propensity of hospital management committees to use funds for prestige projects is enormous. But it is in geriatric service, not in transplant surgery, that the greatest need lies, and hospital management committees should be told so in no uncertain terms.

A Ministry of Retirement

This review has tried to show that there is a tremendous potential growth in the management of the affairs of the retired, not least in the public sector. The number of those who have reached retiring age is growing and the possibility of a falling birthrate may make the situation much more acute. None of the problems we have looked at is at present the central concern of a Ministry of State, but they should be made so. A government department with special responsibility for the welfare of the retired is urgently needed. Youth, Health, Labour Relations, Environment, Sport, Trade— each has a Minister. There is a strong case for a Ministry of Retirement.

The old man in the corner of the room in Saigon was lucky. He had a family to care for him and a social system that accorded him respect and status, even if medically he might not have been so well cared for as his British counterpart.

Is it not time, then, for us as individuals to reassess our own values, to return to the simple Commandment, 'Honour your father and your mother, that you may live long in the land which the Lord your God is giving you.'? It is sound social policy. And in years to come, we shall experience the proof or our denial of it.

Notes on Contributors

The Reverend IAN HENDERSON, an Anglican priest in a West London parish, is Chaplain for Social Responsibility to the Bishop of Willesden and Director of the National Elfrida Rathbone Society. Formerly on the staff of Christian Action, he pioneered hostels for homeless single people in London and Birmingham. He is an occasional broadcaster and freelance journalist.

JOHN DOWNING was significantly educated in Shepherds Bush and Stepney, formally educated at Oxford and L.S.E. He is married with two small daughters, and teaches at Thames Polytechnic. He is co-author, with the Rev. Wilfred Wood, of *Vicious Circle* (SPCK 1968).

JEREMY HARRISON is a journalist. Now a freelance, he formerly worked on newspapers and was until recently Publicity and Publications Officer for Shelter.

FRANK FIELD is Director of the Child Poverty Action Group. He is a journalist and broadcaster, and is the author of several pamphlets.

JEREMY SANDFORD, author and playwright, achieved international fame through his television plays, *Cathy Come Home* and *Edna, the Inebriate Woman*. He is editor of the Gypsy newspaper.

PAUL HUNT is disabled. He lived for some years in a Cheshire Home, and now works as a computer programmer. He is the editor of *Stigma: Experiences of Disability* (Geoffrey Chapman, 1966).

PAUL WIDLAKE was educated at the Universities of Wales and Birmingham. He has had extensive experience of teaching at primary and secondary levels, and has also worked as a Local Education Authority Adviser in Special Education. As Senior Research Associate at Birmingham University School of Education, he was responsible for the Birmingham contribution to A. H. Halsey's Educational Priority Areas project. He is author of a book on *The Education of Socially Handicapped Children* and of numerous papers and articles on the subject of disadvantaged children. He edits the journal *Remedial Education* and is currently Head of the Compensatory Education Department at Didsbury College of Education, Manchester.

BILL KIRKPATRICK, B.Th., S.R.N., R.M.N., R.P.N., Director of Centrepoint, is Honorary Curate of St Anne's, Soho. He was formerly Principal Nursing Officer for the N.W.M.R.H.B., and prior to this Nursing Officer in Charge of the Drug Dependency Unit, St Clement's Hospital, Bow, for the London Hospital Group. He is a sparetime journalist and contributed to the symposium, *Sans Everything*.

JOHN WILDER, Director of the Psychiatric Rehabilitation Association, is a pioneer of community care programmes and author of several studies on psychiatric community health in the East End of London.

WATSON JENKINS is a minister of the United Reformed Church presently working in Wimbledon, with experience of the North and of charity work. A freelance writer and broadcaster, Mr Jenkins is Chairman of the Merton Community Relations Council and in his spare time is reading for the Bar.